Foreword
By **Mark Downes**, Drennan Team England Senior and Under 23s team man...

Match fishing never ceases to amaze me, as it constantly changes and veers off in different directions. One of the most important things I've noticed is how quickly trends change. This is especially the case on today's commercial match circuit.

Here in the UK, we're blessed with some of the best fishing Europe has to offer. Our natural venues have suffered somewhat over the last decade, but many still have fantastic seasonal sport to enjoy. Year on year, our country produces great new match anglers, who thrive on competitions at a wide range of venues.

As a result of the diverse forms of match fishing available to us all, many anglers are now specialising in certain methods. To become a 'master of all' is now more difficult than ever, but when you watch the country's best anglers you see they can adapt to everything. This then raises the question: "How can you improve your basic skills, and become a true all-rounder?"

My answer to this would be quite simple – watch and learn. I have always been a firm advocate of 'watching the greats'. Over the years I've watched them all, from the late, great Bill, ... to the still very active Kevin Ashurst and Bob Nudd. These are all names from the pre-commercial era, but anglers from whom I learnt a terrific amount about the art of match fishing.

I've also taken time out to watch commercial experts like Steve and Phil Ringer, Des Shipp and Andy Findlay. One of the most impressive performances I witnessed involved Steve Ringer winning a match at Partridge Lakes with 90lb of carp. He caught at six metres, alternating between the right and left side of his swim while feeding hemp and meat. This is far from my own comfort zone, but was a fantastic performance to watch.

Getting to the top is never easy, but all of the anglers I have mentioned have one thing in common: the ability to innovate new match-winning tactics and methods. Will Raison, Sean Ashby, Alan Scotthorne, Steve Gardener and Des Shipp are all internationals and all served their 'apprenticeships' on a huge range of varied waters. They all have their favourite styles, but like many of the big names they possess the ability to look ahead, recognise the trends and react before anyone else.

One thing for certain is that you can never fully understand our sport. Every time you go out things change, which is why we keep on going. You need to keep ahead of the game, learn from the best and always be open-minded and innovative.

Mark Downes

| Throughout history, the success of the England team can be put down to anglers adapting to a range of angling styles.

CONTENTS

8 Beating The Best
Who better to kick off with than Des Shipp? Here he dishes out some of his greatest secrets to help you topple the opposition.

14 Seeds Of Success
Northern superstar Andy Geldart demonstrates just how deadly the humble hempseed can be.

18 Baitdropper… For Roach?
Think that the baitdropper is just for big fish? Well think again! Rob Wootton believes that it is an invaluable item of tackle for targeting river roach!

22 Hair-Rigged Worms?
Few anglers are as clever at sussing out a method as Alan Scotthorne, and when he suggests that hair-rigged worms are one of the best, you have to stand up and take notice!

26 Waste Not Want Not!
Adam Richards explains why you should never throw bait away again with a wallet-saving way of winning more matches.

30 Get On The Pellet Wag!
Fish 'O' Mania Champion Warren Martin reveals his edges and secrets that have made him one of the best pellet-waggler anglers in the land.

34 A Seasoned Approach
MAP-backed Shaun Little gives you his three approaches to catch F1s throughout the year!

40 Welcome To The Jungle!
Ever drawn a snaggy peg only to end the day in tears? Let Dave Roberts show you why snaggy swims should not be feared.

44 Catch More Carp
Fancy catching more and bigger carp? Lee Kerry's advice may be just what you need!

48 Playing It Safe…
Tom Scholey describes how a safe feeding ploy can bring you better results.

52 Getting It Right…
Welsh international Andy Neal reveals how a four-pronged attack could be the key to catching bigger commercial weights.

58 The Only Way Is Up!
We take you to Viaduct Fishery in Somerset, where Lee Werrett shows you his deadly lift method for bream!

62 Forget About Carp
Matt Godfrey loves catching silver fish and here he demonstrates why commercial fisheries shouldn't just be about carp.

68 Mixed-Bag Magic!
Fancy a lovely day's sport? Then follow the Sensas experts' advice to catch more silvers.

74 The Bigger The Better!
Maver Match This Champion Les Thompson explains the reasons why big baits are the edge you need this year.

78 Two-Rod Warrior
Commercial-water expert Jamie Masson has been bagging up of late using rod-and-line tactics while other anglers reach only for the pole.

84 Get On The Pellet Feeder
The pellet feeder is a much-underused tactic in Joe Carass' opinion, so here he explains just why you should give it a go.

88 Fantastic Five!
Arguably the country's best commercial angler, Steve Ringer gives you five of his best tips!

94 Keep Them Down
Liners can be an absolute nightmare when pellet fishing in the summer. Callum Dicks has got round this with some clever feeding!

98 The Art Of Dobbing
Mark Pollard has become a master at getting the most out of his swims with just a few slices of bread. So follow his guide to a bit of budget bagging!

102 Sloping Solutions
Sloping venues are always tough nuts to crack, but they needn't be. Check out Jamie Hughes' fantastic tips.

106 The Sinking Waggler
The pellet waggler is a great approach but can be a bit limited in deep water. Here Darren Cox reveals a clever sinking-waggler technique that searches the depths!

110 Method And Margins
Will Raison demonstrates how a simple two-pronged approach is better than chasing the carp about on hot summer days.

Published by David Hall Publishing Ltd. The advertisements and editorial content of this publication are the copyright of David Hall Publishing Ltd and may not be quoted, copied or reproduced without prior permission of the publisher.

Copyright © 2013

Compiled and edited by Joe Carass and Matt Godfrey
Layout and design by Karl Jenkinson
Sub edited by David Haynes and Rob Bradley
Reprographics by Derek Mooney and Adam Mason

WELCOME

Where does the time go? At the time of writing this it doesn't seem like five minutes since the winter months yet already summer is in full swing and the fish are having a good old munch! On the subject of time, we know that commodity is precious to all of you. We understand that juggling your job, family and business is a tricky thing to do, and we realise that the majority of the anglers reading this will not have an infinite amount of time to spend on the bank… and that is why we have compiled this guide!

Maybe you are limited to one session a week or even a month and simply cannot spend much time enjoying your favourite pastime. Well, luckily for you we have employed the help of many of the top names in the wonderful world of match fishing. These guys are out on the banks coming up with methods to help YOU catch more fish.

So, even though time may be tight for you, by reading this book you are sure to become a much better and more competitive angler and, more importantly, will make the most of every chance you get on the bank. We have put together a wide variety of features covering a range of different approaches and venues. The list of superstars is endless and you cannot fail to learn from these guys.

Ultimately, though, fishing should be about enjoyment and by giving yourself the best possible chance to catch a lot of fish, you are sure to bring a whole new level of enjoyment to your game.

My good friend Matt Godfrey and I hope that you enjoy 'The Ultimate Guide To Match Fishing' and we are sure that you will learn a stack of great information from it.

Have a great year

Joe Carass
– Former British Open Champion
– Editorial Assistant Match Fishing magazine
– Ultimate Barnsley Blacks squad member

Joe's Top Tips

Top Tip 1 - Meaty Mush
Feeding meat that has been pushed twice through a meat cutter has caught me hundreds of fish in the past year. This 'mush' produces a cloud that no fish can resist! The resulting mix has been ideal when fished in conjunction with 6mm cubes.

Top Tip 2 - Shallow Solutions
Never be afraid to target fish in very shallow water. Some of my biggest weights have been caught in literally inches of water where the carp could be seen. Start by fishing in 18 inches of water but as soon as the carp give the game away, shallow up and exploit them!

Top Tip 3 - Hollows Are Best
Always use hollow elastics when fishing for carp. Solid elastics are great but the increased stretch of hollow keeps fish loss to an absolute minimum. My personal favourites are Preston Innovations Hollo in 11H and 13H grades.

Top Tip 4 - Hair-Rig 'Em
Hair-rigged worms were one of my biggest edges last year and it is great to see an angler of Alan Scotthorne's calibre also writing about it in this very bookazine! Mounting the worms with a simple Quickstop secures them for several fish.

Top Tip 5 - Scald 'Em
Scalding your coarse pellets brings out all of the flavours and makes them incredibly sticky. To do this simply pour boiling water onto your chosen pellets and leave for five seconds. Drain off using a sieve and bag them up overnight in the fridge. On the following morning remove them from the fridge and the resulting pellets will be perfect for the Method feeder!

Matt's Top Tips

Top Tip 1 - Less Is More
I can honestly say that I rarely find myself introducing large amounts of bait at the start of a match any more. Whether it be bloodworm fishing on a river or pellet fishing for carp, I'm much more confident of getting an instant response from a 'negative' approach. If there's less feed for them to eat, they've got to have the hook bait!

Top Tip 2 - Understand The Trends
Paying more attention to surrounding factors has definitely helped my results of late. Commercial fisheries go through phases where certain baits work for short periods, and to win you must be on top of this. Get on the phone, watch the weather, and adapt accordingly.

Top Tip 3 - A Game Of Patienc
After growing up fishing for small fish, I have a very impatient nature, which has certainly cost me during many matches in the past. When targeting big fish on rod and line, it pays to be extra patient. By this, I mean sitting and waiting on a bomb for up to an hour without moving the bait. When the tip does go round, it's usually well worth it.

Top Tip 4 - Neat Worms
A great little trick that has won me many matches of late is to simply feed neat chopped worms. No end of anglers mix casters and maggots with their worms, and I'm sure fish can sometimes wise up. Feeding pure chopped worms is great for all species, and an effective way of kicking off a swim or restarting a dying one.

Top Tip 5 - Pole Hairs
I have always used hair rigs on rod and line, but only recently have I considered doing it on the pole. After trying it I'm shocked by its effectiveness. You seem to catch bigger fish and miss far fewer bites – a definite winning combo.

It's a pleasure to bring you this action-packed manual of match fishing, where we've got inside the minds of the country's very best anglers.

Nowadays, information is readily available, putting anglers on a very even playing field. You only have to observe the close results of many competitions to appreciate that our population of match anglers is one of the best in the world. High-profile matches, such as Fish 'O' Mania qualifiers, and festivals with big-money prizes are regularly won and lost by just a matter of ounces!

Keen attention to detail drives the very best anglers to tweak tiny aspects of their approach, which is why you see the same faces at the top of the podium every time.

Within this guide, we've got under the skin of the cream of match fishing, draining out every last drop of information to make you a better match angler. Whether competing at club level, entering open events, or mixing with professionals, we all enjoy the competitive facet of match fishing, and constantly want to improve.

New names and young anglers appearing on the scene are both positive signs that match fishing remains strong. This is backed up with the recent alterations in the England senior setup, with Lee Kerry and Callum Dicks stepping forward for the European Championship. Both are unbelievably talented anglers, who are sure to prove themselves on the world stage – you'll be seeing more of them in here!

There's no hiding from the fact that the economic situation has affected angling in many ways, but I think match anglers have played a major part in keeping our industry going. The drive to win sees us out in all weathers, using tackle shops, reading the press, and lining the banks of fisheries. For that, I'm sure we all deserve a pat on the back!

Let's stick together, enjoy the competition and banter our sport brings, and win plenty of matches along the way!

Tight Lines!

Matt Godfrey
– Three times Junior World Champion
– Editorial Assistant Pole Fishing magazine
– Ultimate Barnsley Blacks squad member

BEATING THE BEST

Des Shipp shares some lethal tips to give you that winning edge in forthcoming competitions!

Crumb Crazy

On its day, groundbait can be deadly and I feel I can gain a great advantage by considering how I actually introduce it into my swim. After much experimentation, I can assure you it is closely linked to how much you catch.

A great edge I've gained over the last season is to feed groundbait from the pot, not squeezed into any kind of ball at all. Make the mix really damp and simply cup it in loose. I suppose you could compare it to feeding loose, liquidised bread on a canal.

Being wet it still sinks straight down before spreading nicely on the bottom. This creates a real carpet effect, with a wide, even spread of bait for fish to graze over.

I first discovered this after throwing a bucket of groundbait into a clear River Nene at the end of a session, and was amazed at how masses of fish gathered over the resulting carpet to investigate!

Loose groundbait works really well on shallow lakes, but can also be used on deeper venues. Pushing it into the pot enables you to achieve a similar effect, with the groundbait billowing down before breaking up at half depth. Once the fish are present over the spread of bait, you can revert to topping up with small, squeezed balls, packed with feed to help concentrate them in a killing zone.

This is a super-effective tactic for bream and skimmers, and works on both natural and commercial venues!

Feeding loose groundbait is deadly!

Rubber Revelations

Four main elastics cover me for just about all my fishing. This enables me to get used to my gear, knowing the limits of the elastics and how hard I can play fish, which can be very important in high-profile events.

Starting with the lightest, I use blue Preston No5 Slip for any general roach and skimmer work. Fitting it through three sections means I have plenty of stretch to land big fish, and can tension it fairly tight so that it pings back into the pole every time. I also use this for targeting winter F1s when the going is really tough, as it allows me to scale down my hooklengths, in turn getting more bites.

Stepping up a level, I like light-blue Preston 9 Hollo for bagging up with silver fish on commercials or general cold-water F1 work. For bigger F1s, small carp and all shallow fishing, my red 11 Hollo is brought into play. This is a lovely elastic that's soft enough to prevent hook-pulls but has enough backbone to allow bigger fish to be landed with ease, especially when used in conjunction with a Pulla Kit or Pulla Bung. I'll use this elastic for bream and big fish on natural waters too, when I could potentially hook anything!

The biggest weapon in my armoury is green 13 Hollo. This is used for targeting carp weighing 3lb or more, and I've landed many double-figure fish on it too. Even when fishing up to a snag, I would rather use a relatively soft size 13 Hollo through a short length of pole so that it bottoms out quickly. This way, the fish are far less likely to bolt off when hooked. Remember, the harder you pull, the harder a fish is likely to pull back!

While we are on the subject, let me talk briefly about my choice of elastic connectors.

On elastics below a No6 I recommend plastic micro connectors. These connect your line neatly and securely, and also offer some protection to the elastic. For anything bigger than this I use a Dacronnector. I love these because they give a really direct and tangle-free connection.

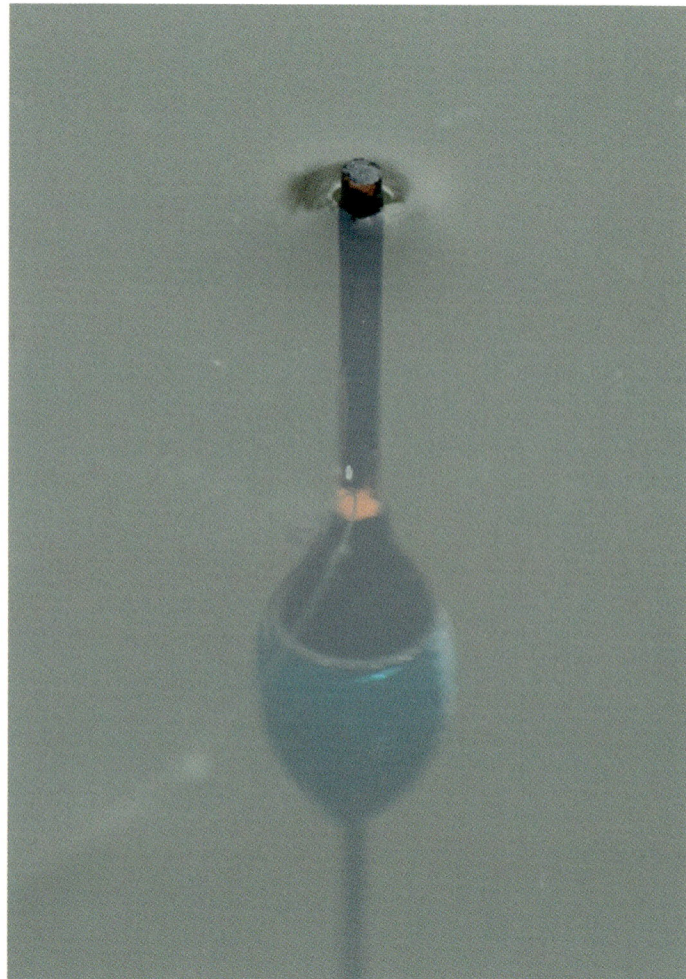

| Dotting his float to a pimple allows Des to see bites others can't!

| Des uses both Dacronnectors and micro connectors.

| Using the right elastic has won Des countless big events.

Baffling Bites

Hitting bites is something I've always paid a lot of attention to. Many anglers miss bites and seem fixated with having a short line above their float. The most common occasion for suffering missed bites is when catching silver fish, especially when fishing shallow with baits like casters. I set mine the distance between my two front seatbox legs – roughly two feet. This is perfect for silvers with baits like maggots and casters. Pellet fishing can be a bit different because you tend to just lift the pole tip to hit bites, so a shorter line can sometimes help.

Quality roach are very clever fish, and the main culprits for missed bites. On numerous occasions I've jumped on the seatbox of anglers who have been suffering missed bites, and straightaway snared some big roach! This isn't coincidence and there are several reasons why I think I manage to catch them.

The first is reading the bites correctly. I've watched people miss lots of indications that I would definitely have struck at. Believe me, some of the biggest fish can give some of the most delicate bites. Often a little dink or sideways movement is a fish with the bait properly in its mouth. Hesitate and wait for that bite to develop and you've missed your chance. That's one important reason why I like to fish with the hook bait just touching the bottom whenever conditions allow, rather than several inches overdepth.

Adding a touch of grease often helps when dotting floats down.

I also strike fast and positively upwards. Anglers in tentative 'pellet fishing mode' certainly won't be able to wallop the hook home!

The final tip to hitting bites lies in the way I lay a rig in. When nuisance fish are about they usually intercept the bait up in the water. For that reason, you are better off trying to bomb the rig down as fast as possible. Don't lay it in sideways; drop the bulk on to the water and follow it straight down the plughole with the float. Moving the bulk down and having just one dropper shot will also help.

These four factors – reacting to tiny bites, striking positively, bombing the rig down and making the rig more positive – all lead to finding those better fish and hitting more bites! Dotting floats right down with a tiny blob of bristle grease is another great advantage in this field, enabling you to see every movement!

Moneymaking Mud

Casters and dendrabaena worms are two baits that you'll often find on my side tray. However, a secret ingredient, responsible for several festival wins, and my most recent £25,000 Parkdean Masters Final win is… mud!

This is essentially just the soil straight from your sack of worms, riddled off into a bait tub before use. The plan is to chop up a big handful of worms, add a similar quantity of casters, and then place it all in a large bait tub with a good dollop of mud. Mix it all together and you get the perfect fish-catching concoction!

| *Quality fish love casters!*

| *The magic-mud approach helped Des win the 2011 Parkdean Masters Final.*

The mud not only helps bulk out your bait very cheaply but it also creates an attractive dark cloud. The beauty of this mix is that you can squeeze it into balls for cupping in so the worms and casters get bombed down to the bottom past any nuisance fish. Alternatively, you can mix it much wetter if you want to create a lingering, black, worm-scented cloud up in the water. Normally, I kick off with a 250ml pot of this mixture, and then leave the swim to settle for at least 30 minutes.

When the time comes to fish this swim you have a choice of fishing up in the water or down on the deck. Both will work but if the fish are showing near the surface then a shallow rig makes the most sense to begin with. After a few fish have been caught you can then revert to a bottom rig. By feeding with a medium or large Cad Pot of bait every put-in you can still keep the feed tight enough to be able to fish both up and down, without spreading the bait too much or ruining your swim.

The beauty of a two-pronged up-and-down approach with worms, however, is that you also catch plenty of other species when the carp aren't there! In fact, I bagged at least 25lb of silvers in the form of F1s, crucians, skimmers and roach in the Parkdean Final on Jenny's Lake at White Acres, giving me the extra weight that put me in top spot!

When fishing shallow, simply ship out to position with a pole-mounted pot full of worms, casters and mud, and hold the pole tip several feet off the deck before tapping out the contents. The bait then hits the surface, creating a fish-attracting splash, while an explosion of bait clouds the water and cascades down invitingly.

The next step is to lower a worm hook bait into the lingering black cloud. On a good day the fish will home straight into this and gobble up the target hook bait. If nothing happens you can try lifting and dropping the bait at various rates. The other option is to keep slapping your rig onto the surface every few seconds. The fish come to the noise expecting to see more bait, but all they find is your hook bait!

Canal Crusts!

I've fished several canal matches over the past 12 months, and one particular bait that has brought me a great deal of success is bread. When the fish are feeding well on bread, it evokes an instant response and can bag you some real specimens.

You generally find that any venue attracting plenty of people traffic to its banks will respond well to bread. A lot of people put this down to the fish being used to eating the leftover bread from people feeding the ducks, but I think the fact that the fish are more active and have to seek out food has more to do with it.

Experience has taught me that the early part of a session is generally better than later on, so it makes sense to target what I expect to be the most productive part of the peg at the time of day that I perceive to be the best. Feeding a firmly squeezed tennis-ball-sized amount of breadcrumb is a safe opening gambit, along with a handful of loose crumb, in the hope that the cloud will pull in extra fish.

As a session wears on, boats will inevitably pass through a swim, in turn disturbing the fish. Rather than worry as bites dry up, be

The initial feed (left) with smaller top-ups (right).

confident in re-feeding, and let the fish settle once again over bread. Many anglers begin to panic and change to fishing different swims with other baits. However, highly

| *Big punches = big fish!*

| *Worm soil lingers in the water; ideal when fishing shallow!*

| Skimmers love bread on canals!

visible bead is often a great gambit in the coloured water after boats. Small, hard top-ups the size of golf balls are perfect for regrouping fish.

One final thing I've realised myself recently is how many bonus fish can be caught when using bread on canals. Skimmers and bream love the stuff, but often slip under the radar of anglers fishing tiny punches of bait! Try using bigger punches, anything up to 8mm, and you're certain to encounter those weight-boosting bonus fish!

Pellets In The Wild!

Having served my angling apprenticeship on venues such as the Gloucester Canal, Bristol Avon and Tockenham Reservoir, I have always enjoyed the challenge of tackling natural venues. Generally, these waters hold an awful lot of fish, varying in species and sizes.

The way anglers approach these venues has changed a great deal in the last five years, with the introduction of baits such as pellets and fishmeal groundbait. Initially, I stuck to traditional baits, such as casters, worms and sweet-smelling groundbait on such venues, but after several seasons of experimentation my thoughts have changed.

Walk along any river or canal in summer and you'll see pleasure anglers using pellets and fishmeal-based baits. While fishing matches on several venues, I've felt that quality fish were present, but I couldn't catch them properly. However, after experimenting with 'commercial' baits, I was shocked by how effective they can be!

One great thing about them is their selectivity. If you get a bite on pellets, it's most likely from a big roach, skimmer, bream, carp or tench… all bonus fish that are worth catching on natural venues!

A great trick on pressured waters is to mix fishmeal groundbait with your favourite sweet-smelling mix too, giving it that little extra 'oomph' to attract the bigger fish.

Pellets are a great skimmer bait. Just like when fishing a commercial, feeding softened micro pellets or 4mms and fishing an expander over the top is a killer tactic. In some circumstances, you can make this tactic even more selective by using a hard pellet on the hook. This is a great trick when there are large numbers of small skimmers present that can be a nuisance when fishing expanders. I often fish a hair-rigged 6mm Sonubaits Krill Feed Pellet. As well as being tougher, a key advantage is that they sink faster than almost any other hook bait, so small fish have less chance to intercept them on the way down too.

| Quality fish in many natural venues have developed a taste for fishmeal.

| The master – happy doing what he does best!

A hard Sonubaits Krill Pellet is a devastating hook bait when small fish pose problems.

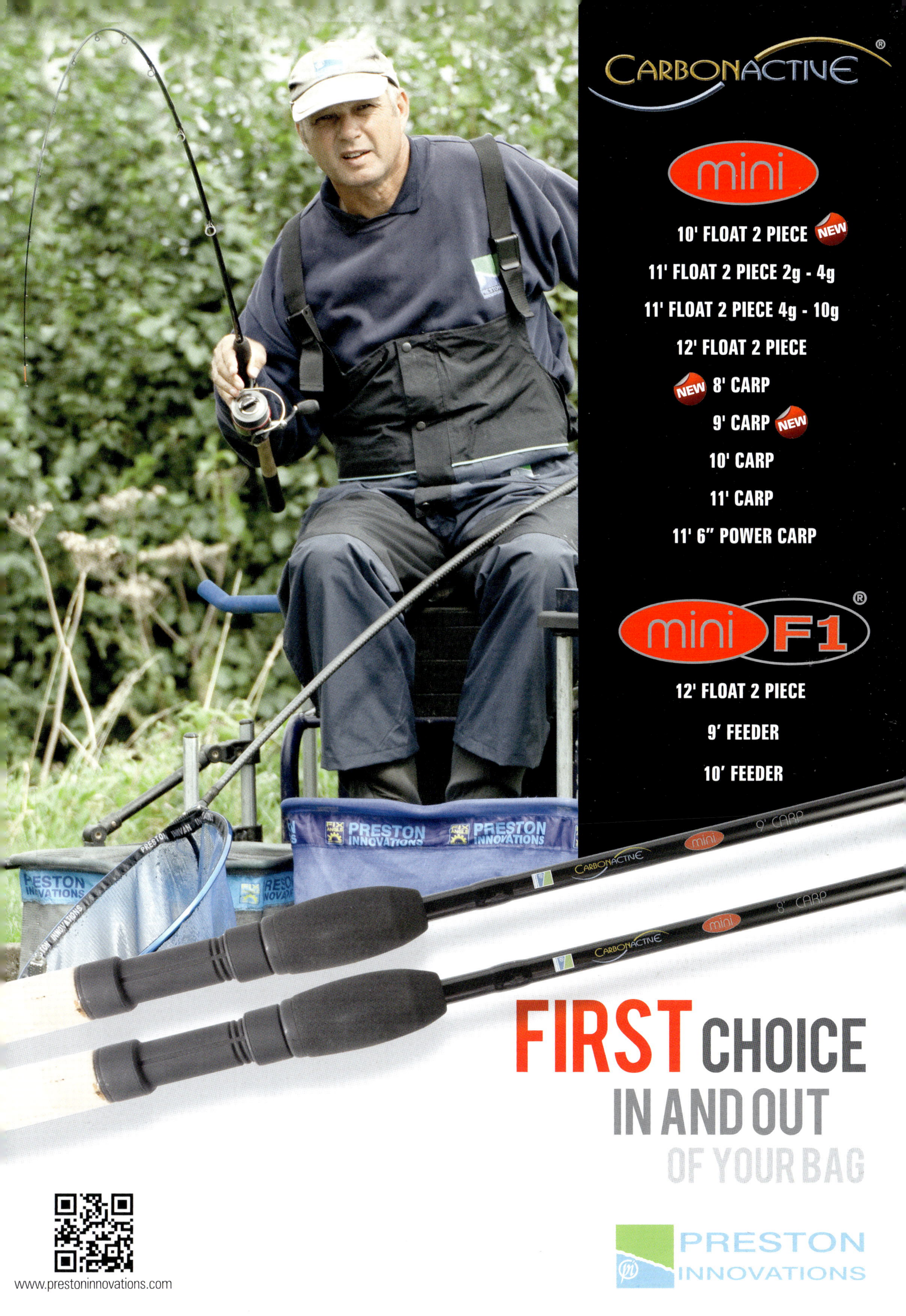
CARBONACTIVE®
mini
10' FLOAT 2 PIECE NEW
11' FLOAT 2 PIECE 2g - 4g
11' FLOAT 2 PIECE 4g - 10g
12' FLOAT 2 PIECE
NEW 8' CARP
9' CARP NEW
10' CARP
11' CARP
11' 6" POWER CARP
mini F1®
12' FLOAT 2 PIECE
9' FEEDER
10' FEEDER
FIRST CHOICE
IN AND OUT
OF YOUR BAG
www.prestoninnovations.com
PRESTON INNOVATIONS

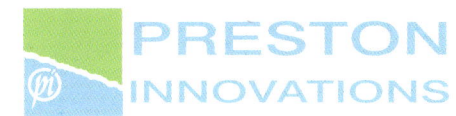

SEEDS OF SUCCESS

Andy Geldart has a long-held love of hemp fishing. We asked the Leeds ace to reveal his seed fishing secrets.

If I could choose one bait to catch a netful of fish on, then it would have to be hempseed. I can't give a definitive reason for this because, like a lot of baits, it is great when it works but on other days you simply can't get a bite on it. The special thing about it is that when you do manage to catch one fish on the hemp, you can be fairly sure that many others will follow, and the stamp of fish are often bigger than average. On its day, this makes 'the seed' a real match winner.

One of the surprising things is how differently anglers fish the bait. Some favour light, strung-out rigs with small floats and tiny hooks. Others are just as happy to slip a grain of hemp on the same heavy, bulked-down rig that they may have been using for bloodworm fishing.

Then there is the way in which the seed is hooked. Some anglers will spend hours at home threading individual grains onto loops of line, which can in turn be hooked. Others like to push their hook through the tough, top part of the kernel then bring the point out of the side. Then there are those, like myself, who are happy to simply wedge their hook in the side of the kernel so that it is gripped by the vice-like shell.

Even off the bank, there are many and varied ways that anglers like to prepare the bait. My point here is that hemp is a very individual bait and, perhaps more than any other, works the best for anglers who believe in it, and make it fit the way that they like to fish.

I have brought the cameras to the Stainforth & Keadby Canal at Thorne, a venue that has shaped the way that I like to fish with hemp.

The 'Stainy', as we like to call it, is famed for its winter sport. However, the time of year when hemp works the best for me is as the water is warming up and many of the small roach that move into the town for winter are migrating back out to the countryside. This leaves behind only a few bigger resident roach and, in my experience, you struggle to catch these fish on any bait other than hemp.

A couple of weeks prior to shooting this feature, I was lucky enough to frame on a big open match here with 19lb of roach, catching nearly all of them on hemp. The venue was going through something of a change and there were still a few of the migratory small roach in the system. Fishing hemp saw me catch a few of these alongside the bigger resident fish and take third place in the match. Interestingly, the two weights that beat me were also taken on hempseed.

Swim Location

A lot of anglers go wrong when they treat their hemp line as a throwaway swim, and put it in a place where they can't present their rig properly. This is particularly relevant on venues that are susceptible to wind,

| Take time out to select a grain that is just starting to split.

| Andy hooks his hemp by pushing the bend into the split.

| A perfectly mounted hook bait with plenty of point showing.

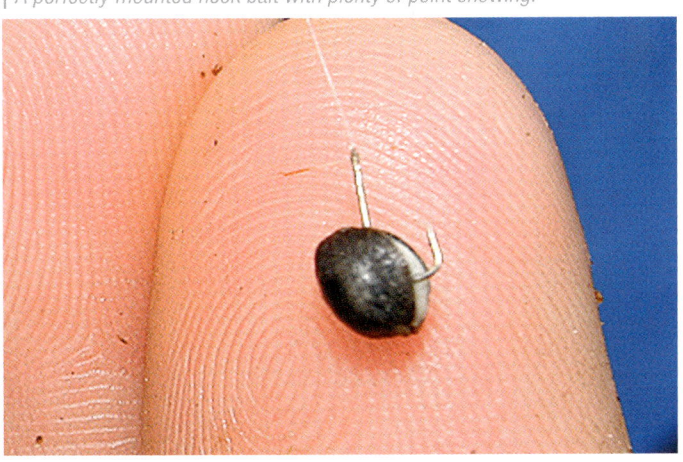

A fine hollow bristle is perfect for hemp fishing on deep canals.

Fishing short allows Andy to feed by hand.

or which can tow in either direction – like the Stainy. Because they don't have a lot of confidence in the bait, too many anglers put what they regard to be their 'banker' swims in prime spots and their hemp line in whatever area of their peg is left.

If I am confident of catching on hemp, I make sure that I locate the line in an area of my peg where I can loose feed easily, and well away from other swims that I may be shipping fish back from. Importantly, I also ensure that the line is fed dead in front of me, so that whichever way the venue flows, I can run my rig straight over the top of my feed.

It is also a common misconception that hemp should always be fished on a long-pole swim. If the water is clear then it is logical to do this, as it would be with any bait. However, in water with a tinge of colour in it there is no reason why you shouldn't feed it by hand, on a short-pole swim, meaning you can catch quicker!

I have chosen to locate my swim just six metres in front of me on the bottom of the nearside ledge. I have around eight feet of water here and, importantly, a nice level bottom over which to run my hook bait. I like to plumb up my rig so that it is just tripping bottom, so a surface that is free of weed and other detritus is also important.

Nurture It!

Depending on how well you are expecting to catch, it is important to feed your hemp line for an amount of time before you go on it. This helps the fish to build up confidence. When you do go on the line there will be plenty of fish over your bait for you to catch!

I know that there are a lot of fish in front of me, so I fully expect to catch on hemp fairly early in the session. Because the fish are here in numbers they will be willing to compete for food. Even as I am catching, so long as I keep feeding regularly, more and more fish should move into the area. For this reason, I will only feed the line for about 20 minutes before going on it.

In tougher conditions, fish may be warier and naturally inclined to spook away from any noise or disturbance caused by fish being caught. In this situation you are as well feeding your hemp line regularly for longer, so that you know that when you go on it the fish will be there and feeding confidently.

Rigs

Confidence also plays a massive part when it comes to rig choice. A lot of anglers are convinced that to catch on hemp to its maximum potential they need to fish light floats and strung-out rigs to give the bait as natural a fall as possible. Again, there is a time and a place for this but the majority of the time you can get away with being a lot more positive.

For 90 per cent of my hemp fishing I use a rig with a strung bulk around 18 inches above the hook and two No10 droppers. The beauty of this rig is that it gets your hook bait into the catching zone quickly, but still gives good presentation through the all-important bottom few inches of water.

Here on the Stainy you tend to find that most of your bites come just after your rig appears to have settled. By my reckoning, this will mean that your hook bait has just reached the bottom. Any bites that come as your bait is falling through the water tend to be from the smaller 'pommies' that inhabit the venue.

On some days, working your float just as it has settled can be a deadly tactic. If you drop your bait in and don't get a bite, try lifting your rig a float length out of the water, then lowering it back in slowly.

When the water is running, you can often find that doing this several times as your rig runs down your peg is a winning method.

Float choice is a 0.3g Garbolino DC27, a cane-tipped rugby-ball-shaped pattern with a wire stem. This is a shape that works brilliantly

This is what it's all about: quality roach on a proper venue!

on deep venues like the Stainy. Although it is extremely stable, when dotted down it is also very sensitive. It is also just as effective when the venue is stood still as it is when it is flowing.

I use fairly thick, resilient main line because when you start catching on hemp action can be furious. I favour fairly robust 0.12mm Garbo Line to a finer 0.07mm hooklength. I have been experimenting with using Drennan fluorocarbon on my hooklengths recently, and seem to be catching really well since making the change. Put it this way, I struggled to catch much here on the individual league before Christmas. I decided to change a few aspects of my approach and started using fluorocarbon for my hooklengths. Since then I have picked up money in every match that I have fished! Of course, this could just be coincidence, but in my head at least it is making a difference.

When it comes to hook choice, I am a big fan of Preston PR 311s.

| Andy believes that fluorocarbon gets him more bites.

These are somewhere between a fine and medium-gauge pattern and offer excellent presentation. Because the wire is fractionally thicker than a lot of other popular hemp patterns, the seed seems to grip the shank of very well. I favour a size 20 for much of my fishing, although I will drop as fine as a 22 at times, or up to an 18 when I am bagging up.

Feeding

As a general rule, you should look to gauge the amount of bait that you feed to the amount that you are hoping to catch. I have started by feeding around 20 grains every five minutes because I am hoping to catch a lot of fish. On a day when I was expecting to catch less, I would feed less bait, as little as half a dozen grains at times.

The most important thing to ensure is that your feeding is regular. This is particularly relevant (and difficult to maintain) when you are catching fish. Don't fall into the trap of thinking you should feed more regularly just because there are a lot of fish active in your peg. If you do, you may find that you bring fish up in the water, which actually slows down your catch rate. Try to set a rhythm and stick to it.

My session couldn't have gone much better. I fished a pinkie swim elsewhere for the first 30 minutes while constantly feeding hemp on my 6m line. When I went on my seed swim I was into fish straightaway.

By keeping my feed going in at regular intervals, they kept coming for the duration of the session. There was one occasion when I seemed to be getting a lot of indications that weren't developing into proper bites and I decided to increase the time in between each feed. I suspected that the fish had moved up in the water due to feed going in too regularly. This worked a treat and these false indications soon disappeared and I was getting proper bites once again.

I ended the session with a 15lb net of quality roach, plus a couple of skimmers. Would I have caught the same on any other bait? I don't think so!

| Andy stores his prepared seeds in an airtight bag.

| Double figures of roach on this superb bait!

BAITDROPPER... FOR ROACH?

Do you think feeding with a baitdropper will spook a shoal of river roach? Think again, as **Rob Wootton** lifts the lid on a very successful method.

Winter is an exciting time of year. It's time for me to really get stuck into the rivers and more particularly my local River Soar. While I do like to vary my fishing throughout the year and fish plenty of river matches throughout summer, it's this time of year that I can really focus on one venue and formulate more specific tactics. The stretches of this river that we fish in matches are as varied as a river can be. One section on the 'natural' can be two feet deep, flowing fast and so narrow that you could jump across. Other parts of the river that have been canalised can be much wider and up to 12 feet deep in places. Although the flow on these stretches can be powerful when the river is in flood, the pace would best be described as steady when the river is at normal level.

I've placed myself on a part of the river that is somewhere between these two extremes and it's this stretch that I like to fish when trying to get a feel for the river as a whole. With around seven feet of depth and a medium pace, the river at the Waterside pub at Mountsorrel can't be described as natural or canalised and, usually, if tactics work here they will work at most places along the river.

Instant Bread Action

During low, clear conditions on the Soar, hempseed works really well and matches are often won with roach nets from double figures and upwards. To be honest, it's these roach that you need to be targeting whatever the conditions. One problem with the hempseed, though, is that it takes so long for the fish to really switch on to it. So, a lot of roach anglers feed breadpunch at the start of the session. It's a really instant bait and can give you a head start on those around you. It's a really good tactic but how to feed the bait set me thinking.

Many guys just cup in a ball of neat punch crumb while others use gravel to help get the bait down in the flow. I've used the gravel option and it worked really well but when it came to the deeper sections I found that I had to squeeze the bread too hard to get it down in the flow. This created a ball that didn't break up and cover a wide enough area for my liking. In my experience, the more compact the ball, the smaller the fish you'll catch, and this was the case. I felt that the area of feed on the bottom wasn't sufficient for the bigger roach to graze over and feel comfortable, so it became very frustrating catching fish that were half the size of those around me. It didn't take long for me to look at other methods of feeding my bread!

Behold The Baitdropper!

After talking to a few guys that do consistently well here, baitdroppering the bait seemed to be the answer – I just had to give it a go. What a revelation! Four of us started to cotton on to droppering the punch into the peg and our results were great. As a team, we won the teams-of-four league run after Christmas and also had top individual a couple of times!

This was, I'm sure, down to how we were feeding the peg. By baitdroppering our punch feed we were getting the bait down to the bottom but also creating that all-important larger area of feed for the bigger stamp of roach to settle over. What's more, the roach didn't seem to mind how often the dropper went into the peg either. This surprised me but topping up with a dropper made no difference to the fish's confidence.

The Next Step

This revelation set me thinking. Surely if the dropper works with breadpunch, it must work when using standard groundbait mixes too? I've since topped up with a dropper full of groundbait over an initial feed and had good runs of fish that I'm sure wouldn't have come when topping up with small balls cupped in.

Now that the weather's turned really cold, would just a dropper of groundbait (bearing in mind it's super-attractive) be enough to start a peg? That's why I'm on the bank, to find out...

| The KC Carpa Gent is the perfect breadpunch float for rivers.

| By keeping his feed tight Rob soon got among the River Soar roach.

The River Soar is a great winter venue!

Three Top Kits

I've set up three top kits. The first houses my baitdropper because I find it so much easier to have a designated dropper top kit set up in the same way you would set up a cupping kit. This means that I avoid having to risk weakening my hooklength on my main rig each time I attach a dropper to it. This setup is simply some heavy line running from heavy elastic down to a snap swivel that will house the dropper.

For the actual fishing I'm going to set up two rigs for just one swim at 13 metres. Both utilise KC Carpa Gents. After shortening the bristles slightly these floats are perfect for running through on slow to medium-paced rivers. The heavy stem keeps them stable and by shortening the bristle they settle a little quicker than normal. I also think that the tip diameter is about perfect on these floats. Some people think that they are too thick but by dotting them down you keep sensitivity while still being able to see them when running down a peg with plenty of differing shadows on the water.

The first Gent is a 1g and shotted with an olivette and four No12 Stotz spread below. By using small No12s I can either use them individually or bulk them in pairs to create a more positive rig. The second rig is the same as the first but uses a 1.5g float. This is shotted in the same way and it's this rig that'll get used if the fish sit right at the top of the swim and I need to get the rig down to them quicker.

Both rigs are made up on 0.12mm Shimano Aspire Silk Shock to a 0.08mm hooklength of the same material and a size 20 Drennan Polemaster wide-gape hook. Elastic for both rigs is Preston No5 through a full top kit and I set this 'pingy'.

Baitdroppers Away!

I'm going to start off by feeding a couple of droppers full of groundbait with just a few pinkies mixed in. I'm using Dynamite Baits Frenzied Hempseed Black mixed 50/50 with fine brown crumb. This creates a lovely, fine aromatic mix that roach seem to respond to well in cold water.

Straightaway I get bites. Not many, but on every run down I'm getting an indication of some sort and the catch rate is passable for the first half an hour or so. After about 15 fish, including a few better silver bream, it's time to top up. Out goes the dropper filled with some more loose groundbait and pinkies and I'm hoping for a good response. It's not worked and despite running right down the peg with a single pinkie (the best bait so far) I cannot get a bite.

Maybe the water's just a little too cold and clear for a groundbait approach? After a biteless 20 minutes I decide to put some breadpunch into the swim instead. This is the beauty of baitdroppering – you're not putting mountains of bait into the peg so can easily turn a swim around with another type of bait.

On the same line goes some liquidised bread through the dropper and the response is instant! All of a sudden it's a bite a chuck again. Stamp roach are nailing a 4mm piece of breadpunch right on top of the feed and it seems that my reservations about it being a little too cold for groundbait were right.

For the next couple of hours I catch steadily and only when bites dry up, or the fish get too small, do I put another dropper of bread into the swim. Instantly the fish come back. After just three hours I've ended the session with a nice net of roach, probably enough to win the section on a match day if it fishes hard. There's no doubt about it, the way I introduced the bait was key to getting the most out of the peg.

I just can't quite understand why the groundbait hasn't worked, when it did so well the week before. Maybe it's been too cold or maybe I should've created a base with three or four balls and then used the baitdropper to top up? That could work, because the extra bait would keep the fish in the peg for longer and the small amount released from the dropper would be enough to just spark up their interest again. It's all good food for thought and that's one reason why I find winter rivers such an entertaining challenge. One thing's for sure, for feeding in deep water a baitdropper offers so many advantages that it cannot be ignored!

What To Feed

01 Add a small amount of red maggots and a few pinkies.

02 Groundbait is then used to top off the dropper.

03 Alternatively, bread can be deadly in a dropper.

A lovely net of fish thanks to the baitdropper.

AERO SERIES

Aero Spin

Aero Feeder

Aero Match
(Double Handle)

Aero... the shape of things to come

X SHIP

X AERO WRAP II

AR-C SPOOL

Protective Line Clip | Anti-Twist Power Roller | AR-C Spool and Line Reducer

RRP. PRICES FROM
£179.99

SHIMANO AERO SERIES - DESIGNED FOR ANGLERS WHO KNOW WHAT'S GOOD FOR THEM!
The **Aero Series** is available in **Match**, **Feeder** and **Spinning** models (each technically specified for their intended use) and feature a wide diameter oversized **AR-C spool** combined with a small compact body. **Aero Wrap II** line lay, for superb casting performance with both heavy mono and ultra fine braid, **X Ship** gearing for efficient winding performance, and a super fine front drag for confident fish-playing deliver faultless performance. With each model you get a spare spool and a line reducer (2 on the Match version) to tailor the spool capacity to suit your line choice. Aero - it's the shape of things to come.

Model	Weight (g)	A-RB	Roller Bearing	Gear Ratio
Aero Match FA	385	3	1	5.2:1
Aero Feeder FA	340	3	1	5.8:1
Aero Spin FA	330	3	1	4.8:1

Line Capacity
Standard Spool — 200m x 10lb (0.22mm)
Shallow Spool Reducer — 200m x 8lb (0.20mm)
Match Spool Reducer (Match reel only) — 150m x 5lb (0.14mm)

shimanofishinguk

SHIMANO
www.shimano.com

See us on **YouTube**
http://www.youtube.com/shimanofishinguk

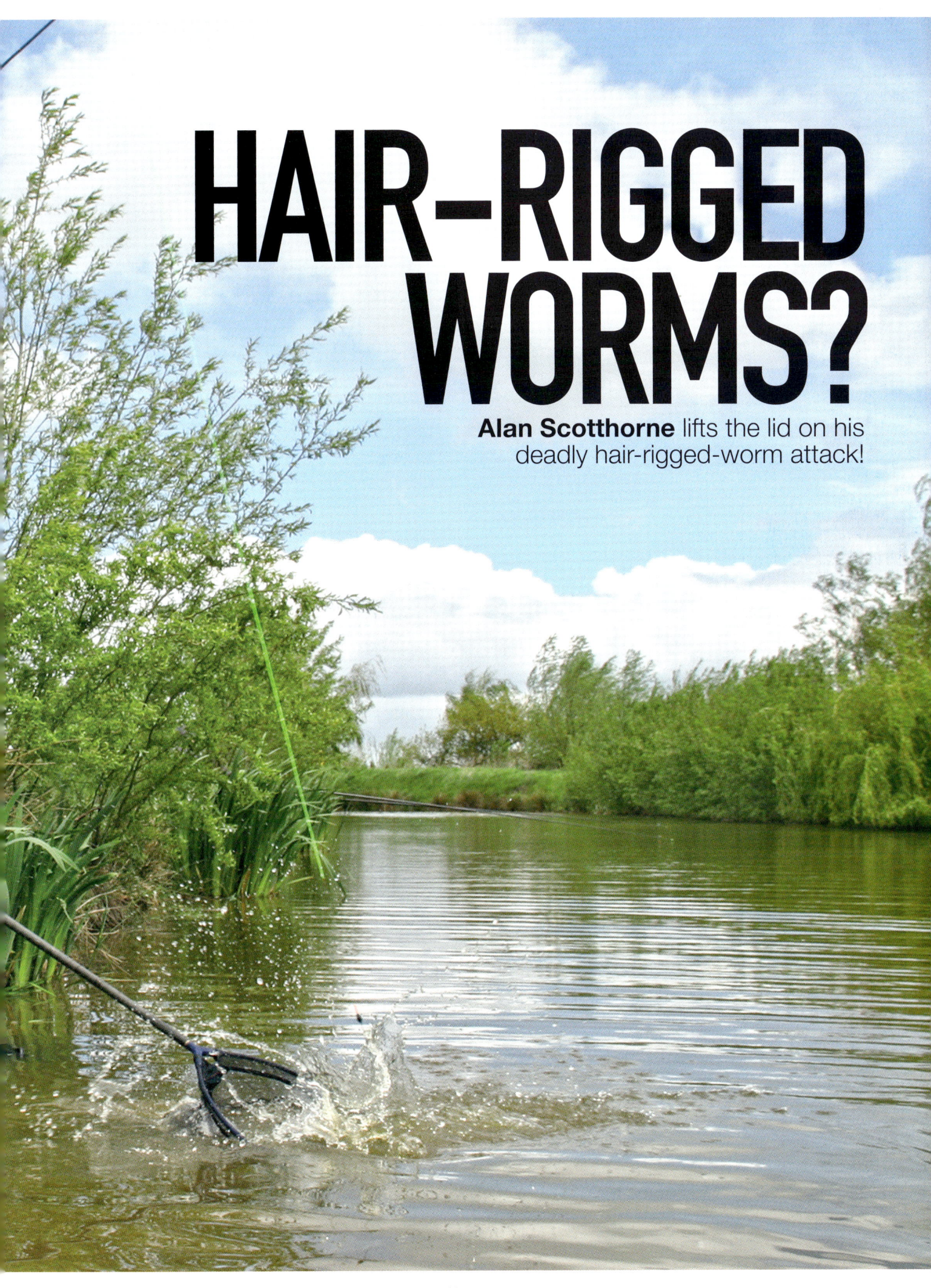

HAIR-RIGGED WORMS?

Alan Scotthorne lifts the lid on his deadly hair-rigged-worm attack!

There comes a time in angling when you just stumble across a method that is a masterstroke! I have long been a fan of hair rigging baits on the pole and since my focus switched to commercials several years ago I have caught thousands of pounds of carp on hair-rigged hook baits.

The use of these is widespread nowadays, with anglers employing them not just on rod-and-line tactics but also on the pole. In fact, I actually believe that using the hair rig on the pole can turn you into a match winner, such is its effectiveness.

I have also been experimenting with presenting baits other than hard pellets on a hair. Firstly I was fishing meat, which was absolutely deadly when targeting carp in shallow water, but what was also good was just how well it worked for F1s. We all know how difficult this species can sometimes be to catch; some days they will literally rip the elastic from the pole tip, yet on others they give the tiniest bite that barely registers. I knew there must be a solution to this and I believe hair rigging is it!

In spring, fisheries start to become dominated by anglers fishing worms. For this reason I started playing around with hair rigging worms. Now this isn't anything new and I can't claim to have invented it, but what I do know is that there aren't many people who hair rig worms. I have since won so many matches on the hook bait that I now have 100 per cent confidence in it and rarely hook a worm 'normally' these days.

Recently I have been doing very well at venues such as Lindholme by using this approach, but one match that sticks in my mind was the recent Drennan Knockout Cup at Woodland View. I drew a very poor area of Back Deans, one that I have drawn several times before, so I started the match fishing a variety of methods in the hope of just catching enough to get through. This saw me fishing pellets for skimmers. This plan just never worked, though, and with 90 minutes to go the exit door was wide open.

I knew something needed to be done and I made the switch to a hair-rigged worm and ended up catching some carp that were almost enough to get me through. That day I caught the carp shallow and actually slapped the worm's head onto the surface to grab the carp's attention. It worked a treat and every bite saw the elastic streaming out from these notoriously finicky carp. Fair enough it wasn't enough to get me through,

| The key components of the rig.

but had I made the switch sooner then who knows?

But what are the benefits of hair rigging worms, and just how do you go about it? Well, for me, firstly it allows you to have a hook that isn't masked in any way. As any angler will know, you often get the hook point masked when using sections of worm as a hook bait and lost fish can often be a nightmare. With my approach the entire hook is showing, meaning the hook-holds are fantastic and lost fish are rare.

Another great advantage is that you can get away with a small hook; if I were to straight hook a worm then I would likely have to use either a size 16 or even a 14, which affect presentation. However, with my hair rig I can use a size 18 B911 and it sits perfectly.

The second point, and perhaps the most important, is the amount of bites that you hit. As I said earlier, F1s can be extremely finicky on some days and the hair rig definitely helps with hitting bites when you are fishing a long pole and there is a delayed reaction to the bite. I have noticed that when hair rigging a worm, more of the tiny dinks that you get are fish on when you lift up, and also you get a lot of bites where the elastic just comes out of the pole.

As far as the correct rig is concerned then it couldn't be simpler, but there are a few key things that must be right. For me the best hook for this game is an eyed Kamasan B911 in a size 18. It is a fairly lightweight hook but one that I have used for years and I know that it is the best pattern for pole work. This is then tied with a knotless knot and on the hair sits a Drennan Pellet Brown PushStop. What is crucial is the length of the hair, and for me a short 10mm hair is perfect.

To mount the worm I simply push the PushStop into the nose of the worm, then once it's threaded up the hair I grip the stop and remove the needle. As you are squeezing the stop it naturally turns inside the worm and locks the bait in place; it is then a simple case of nipping the worm to the size that you require. The hooklength is kept short and I find five to six inches is best.

The rig is ultra simple and comprises a Preston PB Carp 4 float in either a 4x12 or 4x14 size and a bulk of shot just above the hooklength. What is important, though, is how you plumb the rig up. Today I am on Oasis Lake at Lindholme, which is a typical snake lake. The key on here is to find shallow water and today the shallowest water I can find is two feet six inches, and that is touching the far bank. It is a little deeper than I would have liked but, by using a heavy float, it can be conquered. Importantly, the rig needs to be plumbed up to dead depth; I have found that if you lay any line on the deck it increases the risk of foul hooking fish. One final point on my rig is the use of two or three back shots above the float. This keeps me in total control and in direct contact with my float at all times, allowing me to react to fast bites easily.

| Big ide are suckers for worms!

Add a pinch of worms and casters...

...then cap off with groundbait and soil.

How To Hair Rig Worms

01 Insert the PushStop needle into the PushStop.

02 Pierce the worm's head with the PushStop.

03 Nip off the worm to the size you want.

04 The PushStop will turn in the worm – perfect presentation!

Getting your feed right is so important when targeting F1s on snake lakes. For today's session I have brought about a pint of worms, a pint of casters, some riddled soil and half a bag of Sensas Crazybait Gold groundbait. The worms are cleaned off with water and are chopped extremely finely until they are almost soup-like, with the occasional big piece in there. I must stress, though, that this is for targeting F1s and if I were solely after proper carp then I would just chop the worms in half.

The next task is to sort the soil out. This is fantastic for making a cloud in the swim and also helps cap the pot off so that the bait doesn't spill when shipping out at speed. The soil is simply the stuff that is riddled off worms, and I make a point of keeping it from previously cleaned worms. I do, however, add my own twist with a handful of Crazybait Gold groundbait, just to give my bait a fishmeal taste. This mix is then dampened slightly so that it will stick nicely in the pot.

Interestingly I don't mix my casters and worms together like many anglers do. In my mind, adding too many casters is only going to draw in nuisance silvers so I mix it up throughout the day. My pot is then filled with a pinch of worms, a few casters and the rest of the pot is filled with the soil. I feed one of these every cast to keep the swim fed.

To kick my swim off today I have just fed one Kinder pot of bait and have gone straight in with a 1in section of worm. Bites are instant and what is noticeable is how few bites I am actually missing. I have started on the light 4x12 rig and at first it is ideal; however, the wind has been creeping up and up, and now it is a full-blown hurricane! For this reason I have increased my float size to a 4x14 to give me that all-important stability. This is also helping with the deeper than average swim as I am getting a lot of line bites every time I feed.

One problem that is starting to occur is the amount of nuisance fish that I am attracting, so I have cut back on the amount of casters and am feeding more worm. I have also upped the size of the section of worm that I am putting on the hook.

This then highlights the next problem as, when I put a large segment of worm on the hair, I simply don't catch any F1s, so it's a balancing act, and today a piece of about 15mm is the best compromise.

It is soon a case of going through a time-and-motion routine and trying to come back with a fish on every chuck. Getting your elastic right is crucial to making the most of this catching situation and I use a Drennan Green 6-8 Bungee and combine this with a Drennan Pull Bung. Importantly, though, to keep the elastic performing perfectly I give the elastic a liberal spraying of Slick elastic lube. I used to have problems with my elastics hanging out of the pole tip and also sticking inside the pole. This Slick completely stops this problem and the elastic works perfectly all day. The Pull Bung is essential, though, as I like the soft elastic, which allows me to ship back quickly before I power the elastic up by stripping some elastic from the Pull Bung.

Once my feeding was sorted I completely emptied it with F1 after F1 coming to the net. I also caught a few bonus barbel and chub, which at around 1lb each are well worth catching and highlight the effectiveness of worms.

Soft Green Bungee allows everything to be landed.

The session has run like clockwork and what has been noticeable is that I have only fed around half of my bait in a three-hour session.

I think a lot of anglers are put off fishing worms as they have heard all the myths about needing to feed two kilos of worms and six pints of casters, but by feeding the soil/groundbait mix it does away with masses of bait and keeps the bait bill low.

The hair-rigged worm has also been a massive advantage as I have hardly missed a bite all day!

Lost fish have also been kept to a minimum and most of the fish have been hooked nicely in the top lip. It is such a simple tweak to a rig that you must give it a try, as it is a secret that I have been trying to hold on to for quite some time!

| *A fantastic net of fish thanks to hair-rigged worms!*

WASTE NOT WANT NOT!

Adam Richards shows you why throwing away your leftover maggots might be the worst thing you could do.

In these times of recession we all need all the help we can get! As anglers we are often some of the fussiest people around. We cry out for top-quality bait, only the freshest will do. This even sees many of us throw away perfectly good bait at the end of a match!

Over the winter months I used to throw away about a pint of maggots every single week! Every Friday I used to go down to the tackle shop and get my customary pint of reds and whites. This was then wasted when I invariably drew a pellet peg and the maggots were no longer needed. Then because of my fussy nature the maggots got fed to the local wildlife before the whole cycle happened again next week.

As things became economically tougher, though, I decided to pop every amount of leftover maggots in the freezer. Before I knew it I had a freezer packed to the gunnels with dead maggots and I made it my quest to come up with an approach to use them in the summer and get almost 'free' fishing!

But why are dead maggots so good? Well, for me they work along the same lines as casters do for quality fish. Their dormant nature means that a big fish has time to come in and check out what is going on before deciding whether to eat or not. Nuisance silvers are rarely a problem as they seem to much prefer live maggots, and dead maggots remain untouched until a bigger fish comes along.

Killing the maggots is simplicity itself. All I do is riddle off the excess maize from the live maggots and then pop them in a freezer bag and tie them down tight to remove all of the air. I then put them in the fridge to chill them down before finally moving them to the freezer until I need them. Putting them in the fridge and chilling them seems to prevent them going too stretched and pale. If you want to add any liquid or powdered additives then add them before you put them in the fridge and freezer. The whole freezing process will draw in any flavour and make the maggots perfectly flavoured. One tip I can give is to put no more than one pint in a bag – maggots have a nasty habit of coming back to life when stored in larger bags!

But how to use them? Well, as I have such large quantities of dead maggots in my freezer I have found that feeding them positively is definitely the way to go. They are a

They may not look appealing but carp love them.

Adam freezes his maggots in simple food bags.

The action was frantic at Barnburgh!

A mix of maggots and groundbait was fed.

widely used feed for margin work but I use them tight across too, where I actually feel they are even more productive! I combine the maggots with groundbait and feed a combination of the two. The groundbait is a concoction I put together myself that is a finely ground mix of several different pellet types. It's a beautiful groundbait and I have found that it helps to draw the bigger carp into your peg. You don't need much, though, and a kilo is ample for the session.

Today I have come to Barnburgh Lakes, a typical modern commercial that has a wide variety of species to target. Key species are carp, F1s, ide and barbel. All are worth catching and to put together a winning weight here you need to catch them all! I have seen many anglers come to venues such as this and just fish baits like pellets or meat. These baits undoubtedly have their day but all too often the anglers prepared to catch everything will get a better result. This is where maggots score so well. The early part of your match will usually be busy as a procession of ide and F1s come to the net before the large carp muscle in on the act!

To feed the maggots, I simply feed large pots capped off with a small handful of groundbait. This is enough to kick off the swim. I then keep the swim topped up with small pots of bait. Usually this is a medium-sized Cad Pot. In the margins I would feed larger amounts less frequently and look to leave it until the last hour of the match.

On prolific waters such as this three lines will be enough. I will fish two lines tight across to the far side in the shallowest water I can find. However, I do have a trick up my sleeve. For carp and ide the shallow water is ideal, they will confidently feed up there and be easy enough to catch. F1s prefer more water over their heads, though, and usually about two feet is better. With this in mind I will set up two rigs, one for tight against the island in shallow water and the other in two feet. I still feed in the same place but quite often a switch to the deeper rig will see you latch into a few bonus F1s. I will feed a margin line too, situated where I can find 18 inches of water to fish in for the carp.

My rigs are simple affairs. I use 0.12mm Cenex main line direct to a size 16 B911 F1 hook. The float is a 4x12 Malman Cedar and the elastic is a Yellow Cenex Hollow 6-10. The shotting is simply a bulk about five inches from the hook with the rig set at dead depth, although it doesn't matter if you are slightly overdepth.

Today has been a wonderful example of just how effective dead maggots are! I have initially caught ide and F1s but through steady feeding the big carp have turned up! At times the action has been incredible and for long spells the fish have been 'tailing up' in my peg searching out every last morsel of bait. The best hook bait has been three dead maggots but then the carp arrived, when impaling six or seven was good. What was so evident, though, was the need for the other species. I have had a good 60lb of ide, F1s and barbel today and in a match these would have boosted my catch up to a potential match-winning one.

So the next time you are thinking of throwing away maggots, do yourself a favour and stick them in your freezer!

Just the carp from Adam's awesome catch!

Even barbel love dead maggots.

BENWICK SPORTS

UNIT 22, NORTHFIELD BUSINESS PARK, SOHAM, ELY, CAMBRIDGESHIRE, CB7 5UE

Tel/Fax: 01353 721009

E-mail: sales@benwick-sports.co.uk

ONE OF THE LARGEST SELECTIONS
OF POLE FLOATS, FLOATS, HOOKS, LINE AND ACCESSORIES
YOU WILL FIND ANYWHERE!

✓ *Family owned specialist shop, established for 35 years*

✓ *Personalised service, expert advice, so you can shop with confidence*

✓ *Try before you buy on poles up to 16m*

✓ *Large selection of tackle & bait, with all major brands stocked*

✓ *Secure online shopping*

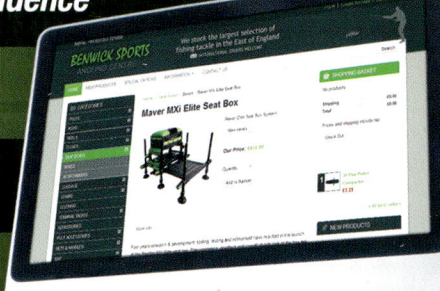

VISIT OUR BRAND NEW WEBSITE

Visit us online at
www.benwick-sports.co.uk

GET MORE FROM THE PELLET WAGGLER THIS SUMMER.

GET ON THE PELLET WAG!

Fancy a crack at the pellet waggler? Then follow **Warren Martin's** guide for summer success.

The pellet waggler is one of the most devastating approaches on commercial fisheries up and down the country. It accounts for hundreds of match wins and when it is working it is extremely hard to beat. However, the pellet waggler as a method has changed.

Once an approach where you would cast out a super-thick waggler and just fire pouch after pouch of pellets at it while waiting for the rod to be pulled from your hand, now the carp have wised up and on some venues this once crude approach has been replaced with a delicate method more akin to a waggler setup for roach!

Firstly, let's look at the basis for this approach and why it works. As we all know, during the summer months carp love to feed in the shallow layers. The pole is a great

way to present a bait shallow and can be deadly on the right day; for the most part, though, on bigger, open-water venues, carp just won't come within pole range. This 'quiet zone' out of pole range is the territory of the pellet waggler and can normally see carp more obliging than on the pole line. Also, in these days when anglers are somewhat obsessed with the pole, by fishing a waggler you often have a large area of open water to yourself. This means that fish can be drawn from all over the lake.

There are three key elements to bear in mind for a successful pellet-wag session, and first up is work rate. It is a simple fact that lazy anglers can't make the pellet wag work. You have to be prepared to make several hundred casts in a session. On some days you won't catch anything by leaving the float in for longer than 10 seconds, yet on others leaving the float 'hanging' for a few minutes is the way to go. You have to work out how the fish want it on the day, as every day is different.

| These Middy catties are ideal.

| Warren relies on two waggler designs.

Here at Barford Lakes the fish have seen all manner of pellet-wag techniques and have become very difficult to catch. They rarely respond to the splash of the float and it is often a case of casting slightly further than the loose feed and then drawing the float back into the bait. If I don't get a bite within 15 seconds then I will twitch the float back a further metre. I give this 10 more seconds and then reel in and repeat the whole process. During this time I will have fed three or four times.

Under the same umbrella as work rate is the depth that you fish. Many open-water venues have a good depth in front of you but Barford offers 12 feet or more. This means that the carp are not always inches deep. In fact, I actually start on a bigger float and fish 10 feet deep to start with! I would expect to catch a few at this depth but it is a good barometer as to where the majority of the fish are in the water column. If I am getting a lot of liners and missing bites I will shallow up one foot at a time until I start hitting bites.

To catch the really big weights you will normally need to catch somewhere between 18 inches and three feet deep but there are days when the fish simply won't come up that shallow. It is all about concentrating hard and responding to all of the indications on the float. After all, they are the only things that truly tell you what is happening in your swim.

The second key factor is feeding. I will always feed 8mm coarse pellets for this style of fishing and tend to bring at least five pints with me, depending on venue rules. It is not necessarily about feeding loads of bait, it is just the sheer regularity of the feed that will see you get through several pints. I base all my attack around feeding three pellets at a time, twice a minute. This creates a constant noise that will draw the fish into the peg and get them competing for every individual pellet.

However, I have found that on some days you can get away with feeding more, and as the weather cools I actually feed larger pouches of bait, but less frequently. It's all about working it out as per the indications but after hundreds of matches fishing this way I have come to the conclusion that feeding three pellets at a time is the best feed rate for 90 per cent of the time.

As I am feeding such small numbers of pellets it is imperative that I feed them accurately. Over the years I have tried just about every type of catapult available. I have found the perfect model for me, though, and have used it for several years. It is the Middy Pro Inter 321 catty that has a big frame, thick, stretchy elastic and a flexible pouch. The pouch has a small disc inside it and for some reason this helps to group your pellets extremely tightly. It doesn't matter whether I am fishing 20 yards or 50 yards I know that I can comfortably feed accurately with this 'pult.

As with any catty, though, you need to make sure that you take several with you as this demanding style of fishing will normally see you get through a couple per match.

The tackle that you use is also of great importance. You need to choose the right rods and my new Matrix Carpmaster rods are just the job. For years I used an old Shakespeare Victory X rod that was so battered I had to tape the reel to the handle. It was the perfect piece of kit and up until now I have never found a rod to touch it; the Carpmasters, however, are miles better and I am not just saying that because I am sponsored as I would still use my old rods if the new ones weren't right!

I use the 11ft Carpmaster for fishing up to three feet deep but switch to the longer 12ft version for depths over this. This is simply because the longer rod means that it picks up the line quicker, helping me strike through the float.

The terminal tackle I use is also especially important. My main line is always 6lb Maxima, which I have used for more years than I can remember. It is super-strong, lasts ages and sinks well when I need it to. It also casts well, which is important as I sometimes use a small, 3BB waggler. I nearly always

Keep the feed regular and tight.

use a 0.18mm hooklength, which I tie to a size 16 Matrix Carp Bagger hook. This is finished off with a small pellet band that is tied in a small loop tight to the bend of the hook. I find that I miss fewer bites when using a short hair.

As far as floats are concerned I stick to two types. For the deeper rod I use a 6g or 8g (depending on the wind) Garbolino Unloaded Pellet Waggler. This is a fairly long float that remains stable, almost like a long peacock waggler. I shot this float with two big locking shot either side of the float and then place three No9s spread out down the line. These register on the float and just give me an idea of when the hook bait has fallen to full depth. Some anglers don't use any droppers when fishing the deep waggler, but I find that quite often the weight of the pellet itself won't sink the line between hook bait and waggler.

For my shallower setup I use a 3SSG Styro Foam waggler, again shotted with two big locking shot. I always place the locking shot on some small lengths of pole-float silicone tubing; this just protects my main line and allows me to pinch the shot on firmly to stop it from sliding. These floats are ideal as they don't dive, meaning that they are fishing as soon as they land. If the wind is bad I would consider stepping up my float size but prefer to fish the lightest float that I can get away with.

Finally, my third float is a cut-down styro waggler that is about an inch and a half in length. This takes just 3BB and is used for the days when the carp are cruising and I will try and pick them off as they swim past. The ultralight float makes no splash on the cast, which prevents me spooking the fish as they saunter by.

As you can see, my setup is far from complicated, but what is important is to get the key things right. You need to work hard to get this approach to work – make it your main method and keep working

A short, cut-down waggler is ideal for 'mugging' carp.

at it and eventually the rewards will come. Gone are the days when you will get a bite every cast; quite often you will go 50 casts without a bite. But as a rule you will then get a run of bites before having to build the swim up again. The fish are often big on this approach and, when you think about it, if you hit five bites an hour you will generally have over 100lb.

Today I have sat on a good peg on the Match Lake at Barford. We have had a few days of heavy rain so I was expecting a slow start. I kicked off at nine feet and had to wait 30 minutes for my first indication, although I was constantly casting and feeding to build up my peg. I remained confident, though, and soon latched into my first bite of the day. For the next 10 minutes after that I had lots of liners, telling me that I needed to come shallower. I immediately shallowed up to six feet and got among a few fish before the same thing happened again. I then picked up my other rod with the styro float set 18 inches deep. This then saw me empty it for 30 minutes before bites tailed off, leading me to go deeper.

This was the pattern and by working hard I ended up with 30 fish for well over 150lb! It wasn't hectic but by working hard I managed to keep the odd fish coming! By following my advice I am sure that you too can reap the benefits of this fantastic approach!

| What a session on the pellet waggler!

A SEASONED APPROACH

MAP-backed ace Shaun Little reveals his three F1 tactics tailored for year-round success!

When F1s were first stocked into UK fisheries, I fell in love with the species. Their willingness to feed, tempered by their fickle feeding habits, always makes for an exciting chase! The key to cracking this species is knowing what baits and methods to fish at particular times of the year. The habits and tastes of these fish change seasonally, so having the right methods under your belt is imperative! For the Ultimate Guide To Match Fishing, I've come out on three separate occasions to help you better understand this fantastic species!

WINTER WARBURTONS!

Bread Feeder
(November To February)

Bread has to be my favourite winter bait for F1s. It seems to be able to catch you carp when all else fails and it goes hand in hand with the water becoming clear. Here at Manor Farm Leisure, the lakes have a very hard gravelly bottom. For this reason, as soon as the water gets cold the lakes go gin clear. This makes the bread even more effective, in my opinion, as its biggest attraction factor is its visibility.

Why A Feeder?

There has been a lot spoken in the past about dobbing bread on the pole. However, it is with rod-and-line tactics that it is most effective here. This venue offers quite large lakes and fish often shoal up well out of pole range, which is where the bread feeder can score! By this I mean a tiny cage feeder filled with fine, liquidised crumb.

Many of you will be surprised to see that I opt for this as opposed to a bomb, but in my experience the bread feeder still draws fish into the peg on the hardest of days.

However, I'd stress that the feeder you choose needs to be small. I am only looking to add a small amount of attraction and anything too big will put too much feed in the swim.

Watercraft

As I said before there is a lot of open water here to explore. I look for a couple of areas and try and get bites from them. Today is a typical scenario and to my left is a small island that offers three feet of water tight against it. There is also plenty of cover so this area is bound to hold plenty of fish.

I can't ignore the open water, though, and with over 10 feet of water in front of me it gives me plenty of scope. Be prepared to have a cast about; the main target fish here are F1s and, just like when you are pole fishing, having several lines can be very productive.

The Setup

My rig is simplicity in itself. I like to use a small three-square cage feeder. This allows me to feed just a nice amount of bread. I simply have this running on my 5lb Maxima main line. The rig has a small float stop above the feeder and I tie a small swivel into the rig onto which I connect my hooklength. I am not too fussed about having a fixed rig as in my experience F1s often give savage bites and can sometimes crack you off. On hard days this is the last thing I want!

My hooklengths are a crucial part of the rig. On some days you want to actually pop the bait right up off the bottom. On others, though, a bait presented on the bottom is better. For this reason I tie up plenty of hooklengths between six inches and three feet long. These are simply 0.15mm finished with a size 16 Kamasan B911 X-Strong Eyed. I then use a hair of about an inch in length and use a Quickstop to mount the bait.

Soft rods are important in winter and my Parabolix STI 10ft bomb is a beautiful piece of kit for this kind of short to medium-range work.

Hook Baits

I use simple 10mm discs of bread and always use the orange-wrapped Warburtons thick-sliced loaf. This is the perfect texture in my opinion and is tried and tested by anglers.

As a rule, if I am looking to pop my hook bait up off the bottom I will just punch the slice straight from the bag. If I fish the bait on the bottom I will compress the bread firmly, which produces nice firm discs of bread that will sink quickly but will still soften up and allow the bait to be slurped up effortlessly.

| *This chap took the bait as soon as the feeder settled!*

Liquidised Bread

Making the bread feed is simplicity in itself. All I do is remove the crusts and put the slices through the blender. I don't look to blend it too fine, as I quite like a few larger particles in the mix that will slowly drift up in the water column.

Also, by keeping the bread quite coarse and just giving it a gentle squeeze in the feeder it will explode out on impact with the water. This can draw fish in from far and wide!

If the fishing is better I will squeeze the bread in tighter, which will ensure that the feeder reaches the bottom intact and then breaks down.

The bread feeder really is a fantastic carp catcher. I have won matches with up to 140lb on the approach, which shows how devastating it can be on the right day!

| *Bread's visibility factor makes it excellent in clear water.*

PELLET PERFECTION

Pole And Hard Pellets
(February To May; October To November)

F1s are naturally programmed to chomping and crunching pellets. Hundreds of pleasure anglers use them year-round, and I'm convinced this becomes an addictive habit, just like humans chewing gum! I rarely use soft pellets, but tailor a hard-pellet approach to catch F1s in spring and autumn. The first thing that I do in the cooler months is scale down the size of the pellets used. All I have on my bait tray today are 4mm coarse pellets for hook and feed bait, with a few 6mms as a change for the hook. A hard 4mm pellet is significantly smaller than a soaked 4mm expander, making it very easy to suck in. It also looks completely natural alongside other feed pellets.

| Pellets appeal to bonus commons and mirrors as well as F1s!

| Lassos are very discreet.

Think Light

I have noticed that anglers who consistently catch using soft pellets always seem to comment on their scaled-down line diameters and hook sizes. Despite this, they still put their success down to the bait that they're using and not the scaling down factor!

I have no hesitation in using a fine 0.09mm or 0.10mm hooklength and size 20 B911 eyed hook. Matched with very forgiving yellow 6-10 MAP Hollow, I can still land fish to double figures, without bumping off any vital small ones. I also make a switch from using a durable pellet band in summer to a more discreet lasso in the colder months.

With my approach, I look to seize the attention of any fish sitting in the warmest layers. A light float helps to give a slow, enticing fall, but it's rare that English weather conditions enable you to fish too delicate. Instead, I use a sensible-sized float, but place my bulk at half depth, with just one or two No10 droppers. I then lay my rig on the water. Once the bulk is set, the two droppers slowly explore the killing zone.

It's amazing how many tiny bites you get just as the last dropper shot settles. These are often fish that have followed the bait down, or intercepted it on the way through the warmer thermocline. In water of five feet and less, the warmest layers are often at half depth, meaning fish can be targeted well off the bottom.

My main float choice is a 4x12 MAP SD1. This has a visible plastic bristle that can be dotted right down. Having the float dotted to a mere

| A rig for the deck, and a rig for shallow – simple!

pimple is crucial because lifting at the smallest of indications can often result in a hooked fish.

Cold-Water Shallow Fishing

I also have a lighter rig that is set around three feet deep in five feet of water. This consists of a tiny 5No11 Mick Wilkinson F1 Ratty, with strung-out shot. Laying the rig flat on the water and holding tight to it creates a very slow fall, triggering reaction bites from inquisitive fish. These are often the bigger boys who territorially patrol the warmer layers. Playing around with the depth on this rig is imperative; six inches up or down can make all the difference between no bites and one a chuck.

A great little tip is to ping just one pellet every now and again. The odd single pellet falling through the water accurately mimics your hook bait. I've even caught on this rig when there's been ice on the water!

Dry Dipping

Hard pellets have an annoying habit of floating for several seconds before sinking. They are also very difficult to squash into a pot when you want to feed small amounts regularly. To get around this, I give the pellets a very quick dip and drain them straight off. This doesn't make them completely soft but simply puts a tacky layer around them. They can then easily break the surface tension and can be pushed into a pot to prevent unwanted spillages.

Cautious Cupping And Cattying

I differ from a lot of other anglers because I feed with a large pole cup, plus a catapult and pole-mounted pot. It can be very easy to overfeed and it's therefore crucial to ensure that you are aware of how much you put in. I'm not a fan of frugally feeding just three or four pellets at the start of the session and opt to feed more like a handful to kick things off instead. This may seem like a lot of bait but carp often hover over bait that they know is present and only pick off the odd morsel falling through the water past their noses – hopefully your hook bait!

I then regularly ping four to six pellets with a catty to create a slightly larger feed area, where the occasional pellet falls through the water to attract the fish's attentions. Feeding this way does spread the bait a little, so tighter feeding with a little pot comes into play on harder days. I simply use a Fruit Shoot bottle cap for my pole-mounted pot, and fill this up with 10 to 15 pellets every time that I ship out. This gives me a small amount of bait to accurately lower my rig on top of. Any fish attracted by the catapulted feed will hopefully be drawn to this small consignment of feed, hopefully following it down and intercepting my hook bait.

Top Tip!

One trick I feel can be important is to use a new, hard and dry pellet in the lasso after every fish. These are fresher, sink slower, and better mimic your loose feed falling through the water, and trick the biggest, wiser F1s!

However, if you're expecting a bagging session, try coating a lassoed pellet with clear nail varnish before the start. This way, you can catch up to 20 fish on the same pellet.

| A messy but deadly combo!

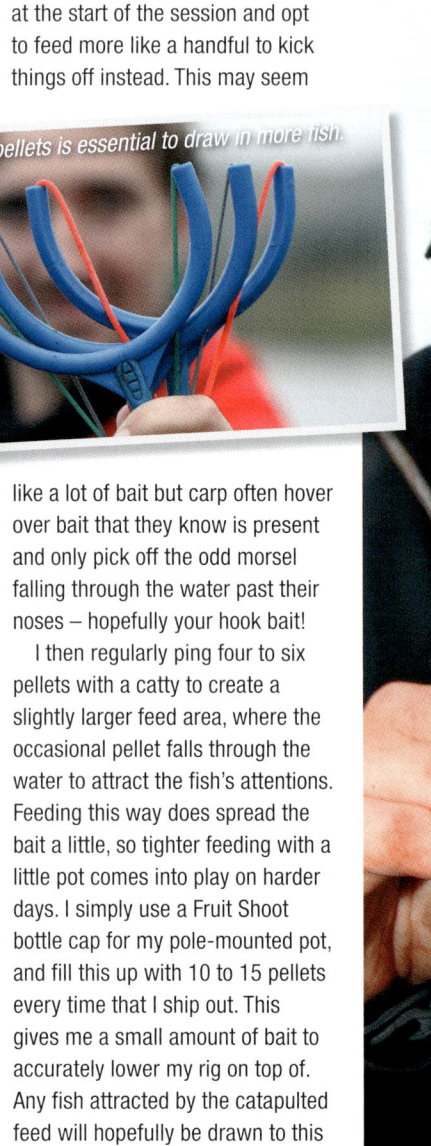

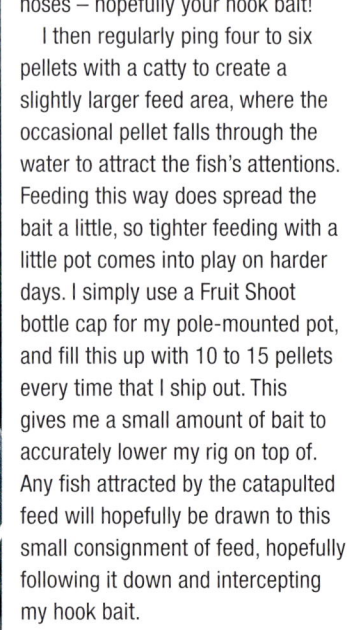

Pinging pellets is essential to draw in more fish.

| It doesn't take many of these to build a winning weight!

SNIPPY SUMMER!

Worm And Caster
(*May To October*)

When the water really starts to warm up, chopped worms and casters are my number-one bait for F1s! Worms are well known for sorting out better-quality fish. They are packed with fish-attracting amino acids, wriggle enticingly on the hook, and have a texture that makes them easy to hook and resilient – the ultimate bag-up bait!

Where To Fish
With the chopped worm, the most important decision is where in your peg to fish it. On most days the fish will be happiest feeding in less than two feet in warm weather. At many venues, this is often found up to an island on the long pole.

At other venues you might not have the luxury of an island to fish up to. In this scenario, your best bet is to try and catch shallow. As with all shallow fishing, getting the fish actively competing is key. I therefore like to start on the bottom while feeding very regularly, then come shallow once I start to get line bites.

Slop It Up!
The lakes here are predominantly gravel bottomed, which is one of the reasons why the venue's fish stocks are so healthy. Another effect of this is that the water is generally quite clear. To make the fish feed shallow confidently, I like to include plenty of mud in with my worms. This lingers as a black cloud in the water, pulling fish into your bait and helping to hold them in the area.

Making my slop is simple. I mix coarsely chopped worms, hemp, casters and a generous handful of soil. Then I add a squirt of Marukyu SFA 420, a potent crayfish and sanagi extract. This is a really effective attractor and adding it to the slop can only have a good effect.

Think Positive!
Fish take worms really positively, so you can afford to fish quite a positive rig. I don't see any real advantage in fishing particularly light lines, so 0.13mm Reflo Power allows me to play fish with confidence. Float choice is an MD1 – a wire-stemmed, hollow-bristled pattern – and I leave plenty of bristle showing so that I can distinguish between bites and liners. As you are feeding a high volume of bait in a small area it is important to wait until a proper indication is seen before striking.

| *Meaty baits like worms and casters offer F1s lots of goodness!*

My rig is shotted positively, with a strung bulk starting at the bottom of the float stem and running to the top of the hooklength. This means that wherever in the water the fish intercepts the bait, you get an indication. To make this shotting pattern work you should lay your rig in a straight line so that it falls as directly as possible through the water.

A soft elastic is also a must, so that the fish swim out of your feeding zone without disturbing the other feeding fish. I favour yellow 6-10 MAP Hollow for this kind of work.

Soft elastic also means that a fine hook can be used to offer a more natural fall to your hook bait. I therefore use a Mustad Wide Gape Power in a size 16 and I'm convinced that the relatively fine wire gets me more bites. Adding a tiny swivel between hooklength and main line eliminates tangles when fishing with worms on the hook.

Feeding
The key is getting into a rhythm so that the fish home in on your feed straightaway. You then just have to ensure that you are fishing at the right depth to catch them.

The best way is to start on the bottom, feeding with both a pole-mounted pot and a catapult to pull some fish into the peg. How long you have to wait before coming shallow will depend on the conditions. If bites are positive persevere on the bottom, but as soon as line bites become a problem it is time to start coming up in the water.

Although I like to cover everywhere from half depth, which is about two and a half feet here, to a foot deep, I am able to do this with just one rig. The water is quite clear so I favour a longish line between the pole tip and float when fishing at the shallowest depths, which helps prevent fish from spooking away from the shadow of the pole tip. Obviously, the deeper you fish, the less important this is, so you can then simply slide your float up and fish with a shorter line between tip and float.

Critical Timing
Although loose feeding casters is a great way of drawing fish into your peg, the key to really plundering them when they arrive is to feed slop through a pot. This gives the fish a focal point to home in on and increases competition.

The most important art to master is dropping your rig bang on top of your feed. This way, you are presenting your hook bait right in the middle of the cloud and bites will often be instant.

When the fish are really feeding positively I stop catapulting bait to make the fish feed even more aggressively. Obviously, you can always start loose feeding again if you feel that the fish are backing off.

| *A tiny swivel eliminates line twist.*

CONQUER THE SNAGS

WELCOME TO THE JUNGLE!

Ever been faced with a snaggy swim and not made the most of it? **Dave Roberts** shows that, with the right kit, snags should be embraced.

Dave Roberts
Age: 37
Lives: Hereford
Sponsors: Tri-Cast, Bait-Tech
Team: Kamasan Starlets

Froggatts Pools
Near Ludlow,
Shropshire SY8 4DL
t: 07967 138150

Despite the uniform nature of many modern commercial fisheries, most will have a few pegs that are considered to be 'snag pits'. Usually these are swims with visible features such as lilies, reeds or roots. The fish seem to be particularly hard-fighting in this sort of peg and can be incredibly difficult to extract from their overgrown home.

Obviously these fish are usually carp but one of the greatest misconceptions is that the fish that are lost are all huge! This simply isn't the case. Whatever the average stamp of fish is in a lake is generally what will be found in the snaggiest of pegs. The difference is that these carp know when they are hooked that they are inches from safety and pull for freedom that little bit harder. It's a bit like a human seeing the finishing line in a race. It still never fails to surprise me how much strength the smallest of carp can generate next to cover.

A lot of anglers shudder at the thought of drawing these pegs in matches but I always see them as potential match winners and set about tackling the peg accordingly.

This style of fishing is not for the faint-hearted and really does require maximum concentration. These fish are cautious by nature and this often means that bites are a bit like a smash-and-grab. The fish will come from out of cover to feed before darting back to safety. As a result, sometimes you don't even get the chance to strike before the elastic shoots out and all hell breaks loose! This is why the angler needs to be alert and ready.

Without doubt, the most important key to success is having the correct equipment. The pole needs to be very strong, elastics have to be set correctly and terminal gear needs to be up to the battering that it will inevitably take.

Strong Poles

The reason why many anglers dread drawing pegs like this is that there is a greater risk of breaking pole sections. I always carry a proper margin pole with me, which I like to use when the snags are within its 8m range. It makes sense to use something less expensive in these danger zones and because margin poles are made stronger there's less chance of a breakage.

If I am fishing long I will happily use my 'proper' Trilogy XS pole. This is extremely strong and has never let me down, but I don't see any point in risking it when I have a cheaper pole that is built for purpose!

Halve Your Elastic

I've heard many theories on how you should set your elastic when tackling this sort of peg. It's easy to get fooled into thinking that you need to use the heaviest, tightest elastic possible, which in my opinion is wrong. I've also heard about using light elastic and striking towards snags, fooling the fish into bolting away from safety. This may work on certain pegs and I've had many fish swim away from the snags on being hooked. However, I don't think it works against features like lily pads and roots because there is only one place that the fish want to head and that is into the cover!

Many anglers shy away from hollow elastics, believing them to be too stretchy and giving the fish time to bury into the roots before you can bottom your elastic out and pull them away.

I have found the best combination to be a half-length of hollow attached to a half-length of Dacron. I'm a big believer in the old saying that 'the harder you pull the harder they pull' and with a tight-set elastic the initial shock of a fish being hooked sends them off towards safety at an express rate. What the half-length of hollow achieves is softness and stretch in the elastic

Small carp are not a problem... their bigger brethren, on the other hand, are!

| *Try to catch away from the snags before venturing into the lion's den!*

Strong hooks and strong line!

Snags should not be an issue if you gear up accordingly!

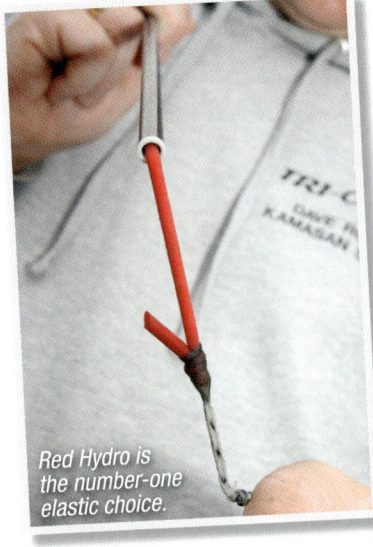

Red Hydro is the number-one elastic choice.

is the key, but I prefer to use a hooklength where possible so that I don't lose my whole rig if I get snagged up.

My preferred choice of hook is a Tubertini 175 but in extreme circumstances I will use Kamasan Animals. Float choice is a Frenzee FP900, which is shotted so that plenty of bristle is left on show to allow me to distinguish line bites.

My shallow rig is set a little lighter to aid presentation. Because the fish are higher up in the water, they have less time to bury into the undergrowth when you hook them, meaning you can get away with lighter main lines.

I still use a half-length of hollow elastic but my rigs are tied on 0.17mm line and hooks are Preston PR 27s tied with a hair-rigged pellet band. A simple inline dibber is all you need and I use a 0.2g Frenzee FD200 pattern.

Importantly, all my rigs are shotted with Preston Stotz because these are a lot more resilient than shot and don't come off the line so easily.

when striking, but once pressure is applied the stretch soon runs out, putting me firmly in charge of any fish. My favourite elastics for this are red Hydrolastic or Preston 19 Hollo.

Beefed-Up Gear

Obviously, this type of fishing requires a beefed-up approach when it comes to tackle. My rigs for fishing on the bottom are made up on 0.21mm Reflo Power and I have multiple hooklengths tied up to 0.19mm of the same. Simplicity

Food For Thought

I like to keep the bait and bites as simple as possible. Paste and meat are brilliant baits for this because the bites are positive, and I'm unlikely to be pestered by smaller fish. As soon as the float flies under I'm already in fight mode, ready for the battle ahead!

It's easy to think that because there's plenty of cover you just feed and fish against it, but it requires a bit more thought than that. I usually start by feeding a metre away from the feature (in today's case it's lilies) with a pole pot to be precise. I will then look to fish between the baited area and the feature. This way any fish that come out from the cover searching for food will find my bait first. It is inevitable that as a session progresses you will end up fishing closer and closer to the cover. Starting away from it gives you valuable time to stop them reaching safety.

If the fish settle over the feed I can usually catch well by feeding with a catapult or by hand. However, I would urge caution about doing this when the fishing is tough. On certain days the fish will be reluctant to leave the cover and will only eat bait that falls in the 'safe zone'. On these days it is important to feed accurately to try and coax a few fish out to feed.

Play Time!

It is easy when a fish is hooked to panic and try to rush it away from the cover. This is where technique is vital. A common mistake is for anglers to subconsciously start striking sideways to almost pre-empt the impending battle. It is the nature of these pegs to suffer hook-pulls because everything is under so much more pressure, and a side strike will increase this risk. Striking upwards will give the best chance of a decent hook-hold.

Once a fish is hooked, the pole then has to be angled away from the snag. This has to be done quickly but in a smooth manner; panicking will cause breakages. Rather than a sudden burst, progressive power needs to be applied in a continuous motion. I have found that force needs to be applied at an angle of about 45 degrees to the water. This not only puts pressure on the fish in the opposite direction it is heading but also applies upwards pressure at a time when it's trying to get its head down.

It is important to keep the pressure on until the fish is guided safely away from danger. Stopping to check where the fish is will only result in letting it turn back with renewed energy. There is no room for being tentative. All the action happens in a split second but being smooth is more important than being quick. Faith in your equipment is essential!

Once the fish is manoeuvered away from danger it is merely a case of shipping back and playing the fish to net. Fish can usually be netted quite quickly after the initial battle due to the energy already expended.

The Result

As expected, the fish have fed freely but my approach has proved very successful at overcoming some extremely hard-fighting fish! I fished a paste line against the lilies, which has given me a real white-knuckle ride, but I've come out of it unscathed!

I've changed my hooklength twice due to wear and tear, but I haven't suffered one breakage despite catching well in excess of 70lb. Importantly, the pole, elastic and rig have lasted a whole session, which proves that my gear is up to the job. If I'm lucky enough to draw this peg in a match I'm confident that my gear is man enough for a bit of jungle warfare!

FISH LIKE A PRO

TRILOGY Pro 2
ICONIC Pro

THE TRILOGY PRO 2 & ICONIC PRO ARE HERE

Released for the 2013 season, these poles from Tri-Cast have taken pole technology and fishing to another level. These poles have broken new ground with the use of a new hi-tech material which incorporates ultra-low resins infused throughout the high-modulus carbon fibres. Combining this new material with a revolutionary production process has produced never-seen-before results. These poles are even lighter, stiffer and much more responsive than ever before, even at the longer lengths.

All of these vital elements plus the use of new mandrels and steeper tapered kits contribute to vast improvements in the poles' overall balance, slim diameter and, of course, Tri-Cast's renowned strength. With a massive and improved spares package, which can be tailored to the angler's requirements, Tri-Cast has not just improved its poles, but taken them to a far higher level.

Tri-Cast offers a complete range of the highest-quality, British-made tackle available for today's modern angler.

	TRILOGY PRO 2	ICONIC PRO
R.R.P	£3249.99	£2329.99
PROMO PRICE	£2249.99	£1549.99
LENGTH	16.5m	16.5m
ELASTIC RATINGS	0 - 16s	0 - 16s
SPARES PACKAGE	1 x Match Top 4 Kit, 3 x Match Top 3 Kits, 3 x Big Bore Power Top 2 Kits, 1 x Short No 3 Section, 1 x 80cm Short Mini Butt, 1 x Cupping Kit for Match Kits, 1 x Cupping Kit for Power Kits and 2 x Cups, Angler's Towel, Cap, Deluxe Holdall	
OFFERS	FREE OF CHARGE – CHOOSE EITHER AN EXTRA MATCH TOP 3 OR BIG BORE TOP 2 KIT	

THE ALL NEW TRILOGY XRS POWER MARGIN 9M

CHECK OUT VIDEOS OF OUR LATEST PRODUCTS ON YouTube AND OUR WEBSITE

When it comes to margin poles, then, as the saying goes, nobody does it better. Tri-Cast has swept the competition aside over the past years, winning Margin Pole Of The Year with the XRS (Xtra Reinforcing System) margin pole – so this new model must be something special. Now using the new revolutionary Trilogy hi-tech material and enhancing it with our very own XRS, this new margin pole is even lighter, stiffer and stronger than before. It comes as standard at nine metres but is that good that we have been able to produce not one but two extensions to take it to 10.6 and 12.2 metres. Supplied with a spare Big Bore top 2 kit and comes complete with its very own padded pole bag this has to be the margin pole any serious angler should have.

ELASTIC RATINGS FROM 8s - 25s
RRP £399.99
PROMO PRICE £329.99

For the very latest news and developments, along with comprehensive details of all our products, please visit our new website:

www.tri-castfishing.co.uk

TRI-CAST COMPOSITE TUBES LTD, WATSON WORKS, DUKE STREET, ROCHDALE OL12 0LT
T: +44 1706 861 807 F: +44 1706 643 336 E: sales@tri-castfishing.co.uk

TRI-CAST
EVOLVING CARBON FIBRE TECHNOLOGY

CATCH MORE CARP THIS SUMMER

Hayfield Lakes
Doncaster DN9 3NP
t: 01302 864555
w: www.hayfieldlakes.co.uk

Lee Kerry
Age: 30
Lives: Leeds
Sponsors: Preston Innovations, Sonubaits
Team: Ultimate Barnsley Blacks

CATCH MORE CARP

Lee Kerry provides you with his top tips to help you catch more carp…

Increase Your Length!

The Method feeder is one of the best approaches for catching carp – end of! However, it has been used to death and many of the nation's carp are becoming wise to the presentation that the Method offers. To counteract this, one of the biggest changes you can make is to your hooklength.

Most anglers go down the tried and tested route of using a 4in trace. Some may use even shorter and I know many of the pioneering Method anglers used hooklengths as short as two inches. I have tried using these short traces where rules allow and for me they just aren't right.

| *Try a longer hooklength.*

I believe that a longer hooklength is a massive edge and can help you catch some of the bigger and wiser carp that inhabit our commercials. I think that these bigger fish have learnt what a Method feeder is and will hang back and just slurp up the bait from a distance rather than eat the bait straight from the frame. With this in mind, a longer hooklength gives the fish more chance to suck in your hook bait from a distance. Now I almost always use 5in hooklengths but will even use 6in versions if I'm looking for particularly big fish.

Pimp Your Feed

Most anglers these days rely solely on using pellets around their Method feeders. And quite rightly so; pellets are without doubt the best feed for around the Method, and although groundbait can have its day, pellets are far more consistent.

For most anglers this means using standard 2mm fishery pellets with perhaps a dash of Stikki Pellet powder to ensure they stick nicely around the feeder. Now don't get

Various hook baits can be productive.

me wrong, you will catch loads of fish using this but you can definitely improve things further.

I am a big fan of the Sonubaits Flavour Shakers and have used them for many different situations. One of my favourite uses is to sprinkle a generous amount onto my Method-feeder pellets. I still prepare them the same with some Stikki Pellet, but will also coat the pellets in one of the powders.

My favourite is the Super Krill; this is an extremely popular flavour and for good reason, as carp absolutely love the stuff! This powder also gives your pellets an orangey hue, which is no bad thing!

| *Carp such as this are clever and need to be outwitted.*

Think About Your Hook Baits

The fairly standard approach is to use a hard 6mm or 8mm banded pellet. Now this is great when targeting small fish or for carp that receive very little in the way of angling pressure. For fish that have seen it all before, though, you need to look at your hook baits in a little more detail. There is certainly still a place for hard baits but, in my opinion, softer offerings should not be ignored.

I have been experimenting with S-Pellets. These are a kind of firm expander that are drenched with oil and they seem to work an absolute

Slapping can bring success when fishing shallow.

Soft rods are essential for carp fishing.

treat. They are a bit lighter than hard pellets and can be sucked up with ease.

Another bait I rate highly for Method work is expander pellets. Now these are obviously extremely soft and need to be used carefully, but they are an awesome bait and really can get you more bites. Their strength as a bait choice is their weight, or lack of it, as they are simply effortless for a carp to suck up and eat. Be careful when moulding your Method, though, and it can be a good idea to pop your hook bait in last so it isn't damaged.

Finally you should never ignore a bright, in-your-face boilie. I actually don't use boilies, though, and prefer Band'ums, which come in a huge range of colours and flavours. My favourites are the white and red options but I also take yellow and orange. These are particularly effective in clear water where the fish are not really feeding and you are just trying to get the carp's attention. A bright boilie in this situation is a sure-fire winner!

Soft Rods

Rod choice is very much a personal thing and what is right for one person may not be right for the next. However, I can only pass on my findings and when it comes to carp, I love to use a soft rod! Where possible I will use the 9ft or 10ft Mini F1 feeder rods. These are superb rods that have gorgeous actions and bend right through.

One of the main problems we have is lost fish; hook-pulls at the net can be a nightmare, particularly when catching F1s. A rod such as this really does help your cause and will keep fish losses to a minimum. But don't just think that this rod is only for F1s, the softer action is great for carp too!

If I have to cast a little bit further then I opt for the standard 10ft or 11ft Mini. These just have a little bit more power that allows feeders to be cast a bit further. But where possible, the Mini F1 rods are my first choice – no matter what the size of fish.

Master The Margins

The margins play a vital role in winning on commercials and it is an area that I have exploited many times over the past few years. I have found that there are key depths in which you must fish to get the most from the swim. I think that depth is more important than cover and will plumb the swim extensively to find what I am looking for.

After much experience I have found two and a half feet of water to be the best depth when fishing for pressured carp. It's deep enough for the carp to come into undetected, but it isn't too deep so that you get linered to death. There are also times when you need to go into really shallow water, usually when there are a lot of fish to catch on the real red-letter days.

The ideal situation would be a flat bottom, but this is extremely rare so it's usually a case of making the best of it. Plumb up and try to find a slowly steeping bottom. Slopes are great to present a bait on and fish seem to enjoy feeding on them too.

Margin Bait

For me there are only two baits to consider for margin work: groundbait and corn. The effectiveness of groundbait as a feed is well documented and it certainly is a popular approach. Nevertheless it is effective and it makes catching

A lovely carp caught slapping.

Try adding powdered additives to your Method pellets.

Shallow Slapper!

My final bit of advice is for shallow fishing. As we all know, shallow fishing can be absolutely devastating in the warmer months and pellets are one of the best baits for shallow fishing.

Gone are the days, though, of simply spraying pellets everywhere and hoping for a fish – it seems that a much better response is gained by pinging just three or four pellets and trying to starve the fish on to the hook.

One of the best ways to get bites when fishing shallow is to slap your rig. Slapping is basically imitating the loose pellets hitting the surface and is a way to constantly 'ring the dinner bell'. To do this, simply rotate your pole so that the rig is flicked over in an almost windmill-like fashion. Repeat this two or three times and then allow the rig to settle. Normally a bite will come as soon as the float settles.

Vary the amount of times that you slap, keep it in tune with your feeding and you are sure to reap the rewards with some big shallow-caught carp.

| *Follow Lee's advice for nets of carp like this!*

down the edge relatively easy.

My mix is Supercrush Expander, which is pure crushed pellets, and when mixed fairly damp it's quite heavy and sinks straight to the bottom when cupped in loose.

This is important; carp create a lot of disturbance when they come into the swim and the last thing you want is a lightweight groundbait flying everywhere and ruining your peg. Ideally you want the bait to cloud slightly when the carp comes into the swim before settling straight back down again.

Feeding is relatively simple and I tend to kick off my peg with three pots. I will only feed this line with two hours to go as I'm sure the carp associate the large amount of groundbait with anglers packing away.

I do feel, though, that it is vital to add some feed to your groundbait, and corn is my number-one choice. Again the weight of corn works in your favour and can help reduce line bites and foul-hooked fish. The particles in your peg also prevent the carp from becoming too pre-occupied on the groundbait.

Having some corn in the swim is great because double corn is one of the very best margin hook baits there is. Not only is it very heavy, it is also very visible – I have caught countless carp on double corn!

FEEDING EXPLAINED

PLAYING IT SAFE...

Tom Scholey explains how a 'safe' feeding approach will win you more money.

When asked what the most important match fishing skill to master is, most top anglers simply reply: "Feeding."

Despite this, it is an aspect of angling that is very easily overlooked. It is all too easy to assume that, because you are getting a few fish, you are doing it right when, in actual fact, by refining your approach you could be catching an awful lot more.

Through my work as an angling journalist, I have been fortunate enough to fish with some of the best match anglers in the country and, believe me, unless they are absolutely bagging they rarely feed in the same way throughout a session. They know how they need to change the way they feed to pull fish into their peg, get them feeding confidently and then plunder them!

In a lot of ways, successful feeding is all about good decision making, and involves weighing up the risks – and potential benefits – of a strategy before employing it. Hopefully, some of the lessons that I have learnt can also help you to put more fish in your net.

Read The Water!

It is all well and good working to a plan, but in order to get the best from a given peg it is very important to approach the swim with an open mind. Rather than feeding in a set way and hoping that the fish respond to it, you should always look to work out how the fish want to feed, then tailor your feeding to suit the job in hand. You can then analyse how the fish respond on a given day to help you work out how to maximise the amount that you can catch.

A lot of anglers (myself included) can get a little gung ho at times, and when things aren't going right it is all too easy to fall into the trap of trying to force the issue, such as by potting in a large cup of bait to try and make the fish feed. Before doing something like this, however, it is well worth asking yourself whether it is actually the right thing to do, or whether you are in fact taking an unnecessary gamble.

After all, we know that fish naturally come on to the feed at certain times of day, so is that big pot of bait really going to encourage them to do so? Or is it just cutting down your chances of catching many fish until they do switch on? Ex-England ace Denis White came up with what I believe to be one of the best rules to remember when it comes to feeding, when he said:

| Micro pellets – great holding bait.

| Tom loves Preston Chianti floats.

"You can put it in, but you can't take it out." Obvious yes, but all too easily forgotten when on the bank.

Tools For The Job!

For the purposes of this feature I am going to focus on pole fishing, and when it comes to feeding we have three key tools at our disposal. These are the pole cup, the catapult and the pole-mounted pot. Knowing when to use each one really is the key to getting the most from your peg.

A venue that has helped me to learn a lot about feeding is Lakeside Fishery, near Ranskill. This place is absolutely teeming with fish but they are not always easily fooled, and the difference between the anglers who have got it right and those who haven't is always apparent at the weigh-in.

Recently, I fished a match at Lakeside where I felt that I got my feeding pretty much right. Hopefully by talking you through my day, I can help you to understand the decisions that I made and, most importantly, give you an insight into why I made them.

When it comes to bait choice Lakeside is very much a confidence venue. Pellets, casters, maggots and worms all work well on their day,

| The locals refer to a big ide like this as a "Doris!"

Tom Scholey
Age: 26
Lives: Daventry
Sponsors: None
Team: Matrix Dynamite Trentmen

Lakeside Fishery
Ranskill, South Yorkshire
DN22 8LW
t: 01777 818524
w: www.lakesidefishery.net

and in the warmer months, meat also comes into play. The venue has a massive head of skimmers, which form the bulk match weights of most anglers, as well as a big population of ide, carp and smaller silver fish such as roach and perch.

Given the vast array of species on offer, I try to be as unselective as possible, and in the warmer months almost always opt for a chopped-worm-and-caster attack. Whatever the bait, though, the following observations about feeding hold true.

Starting The Session

The great thing about commercial fisheries is that you generally know that there are a lot of fish in front of you. In many respects you have a 'captive audience', and so any thoughts of feeding a large quantity of bait to draw fish into your peg and hold them there, as you might do on, say, a big river or reservoir go out of the window.

In the warmer months, there is also little point in feeding lots of different lines (unless you have

| Loose feeding casters is key.

other factors, such as a silty lake bed to contend with). At Lakeside, I generally feed just two: a main line in front of me, and a throwaway margin line, which I will generally only have a look on if I need to catch carp.

On whatever line you plan on starting, feed just enough to get a bite. At Lakeside, this is generally a Kinder pot full of bait. Chopped worm is a great attractor, so I always make my initial feed particularly rich in worm, with a few casters mixed in with it.

Within just a couple of minutes of

| Chopping worms in a pole pot makes the whole process more efficient.

| All species will take a worm head.

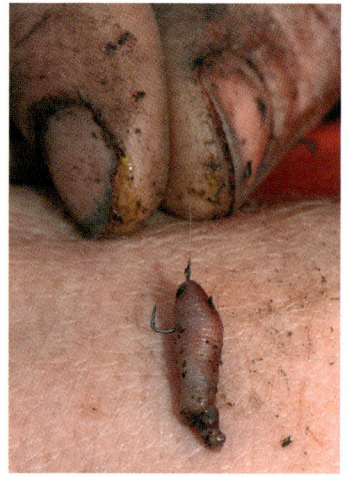

the start of the match a sharp bite saw my first fish of the day come to the landing net. It was a good one too – an ide of about 3lb, and a welcome start. Starting off with just a tiny amount of bait in this way often brings pleasant surprises. In daylight hours, the biggest fish in a commercial fishery are often also the wariest, and back away from big piles of bait on the bottom. A smaller offering presented at the start of the match can often prove irresistible, though, and give you a welcome early lead over the competition.

With a quality fish in the net while other anglers were still cupping their bait in, I had already swung the odds in my favour. I decided to repeat the process, and was soon into another, smaller ide. Three more fish in the next 15 minutes, and I was into a nice rhythm, while others on the lake were still waiting for fish to move over their initial salvo of bait.

By the end of the first hour, I was confident that there were a few fish in front of me, and the fact that I wasn't having to wait too long for bites told me that they were feeding confidently. That said, the time I was waiting between fish was gradually increasing, and with other anglers around the lake also starting to catch, the time was right to up the ante.

Alongside my usual Kinder pot after every fish, I now started spraying around 20 casters by catapult over a 3m-square area every five minutes as well. I hoped to achieve a couple of things by doing this. Firstly, I wanted the sight of bait falling through the water to draw fish in from the surrounding area, and secondly I wanted to create a large bed of bait on the bottom.

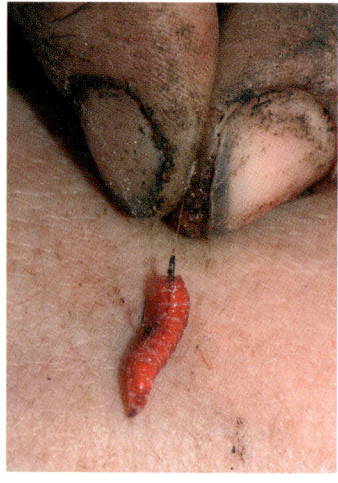

| Red maggot is a good change bait.

This way, any fish that might spook away from my concentrated area of feed when I hooked a fish would not bolt completely out of the peg, but instead hang around the larger bed of bait feeding on the odd caster.

This kept me in business, and through the second and third hour I kept the fish coming as well as anybody I could see. The only slight concern I had was that Andrew Morley, the angler on the peg to my left, had caught four carp by casting down into the corner. The fish were only small compared to the usual stamp at Ranskill, giving him around 20lb, which I reckon was around the same as I had, but there was every chance the bigger fish could switch on for him as the day went on.

Build Your Weight!

In any match, the middle couple of hours are crucial. These are the times that make the difference between an okay performance and a money-winning one. Having seen Andrew catching carp, it would have been all too easy to take a gamble and target them, rather than plodding on with the silver fish. Being realistic, though, nobody except Andrew in his corner peg had caught one by that point, so time spent sitting for them would be time wasted. After all, with the stamp of silver fish that I was catching, it would only take seven or eight fish to cancel out the weight of a carp, so I decided to play it safe and guarantee myself a decent weight.

As the penultimate hour approached, something strange happened. Instead of the regular bites that I was enjoying previously, I was blighted with line bites, and even foul hooked and lost a couple of fish. It seemed the fish were starting to come up in the water – which is the only downside to regularly catapulting bait as I had been doing. Once again, I faced a decision – should I pick up a shallow rig and increase my loose feeding to try and catch the fish up in the water, or cut out loose feeding altogether to force the fish back on to the bottom?

Again, it was the risk factor that made my mind up. With the lake only being relatively shallow, fishing shallow is rarely successful in the matches at Lakeside, whereas sensible feeding on the bottom is a much better bet for a few more fish. This is where the big pole pot comes into play.

First, I stopped feeding altogether to try and give my swim chance to settle down. I caught a couple more small fish without introducing any more feed, before deciding that the time was right to introduce some more bait by pole cup. I cupped in three times the amount that I was feeding through the Kinder pot, before going straight over the top with a pole rig.

This proved a successful ploy, and for the next 40 minutes I enjoyed my best run of fish of the day. I found that I could catch around three fish off each pot of bait before topping up, and although I waited slightly longer for bites, the fish were of a better stamp.

Unfortunately for me, Andrew was also catching really well, fishing into the corner, and it was getting to the point where it would be virtually impossible to catch him up with silver fish alone.

To use another popular angling saying, it is very important to "buy a ticket" and give yourself a chance of winning the match – so for the first time, I decided to have a look on my margin line. After five minutes I had just a couple of small skimmers to show for my efforts, though, and I was keen not to allow the ticket to become too expensive! So, I fed the margin line again, and went back out on my silver-fish swim. I would always rather give myself a good chance of achieving a frame position, than go all out to win and leave empty-handed.

As we moved into the final hour, my silver-fish line became stronger and stronger, and with the fish feeding extremely confidently, big potting was definitely the most effective way of feeding.

At the end of the match, I expected I have around 50lb and was pleased when the scales arrived and gave me 58lb 6oz. This was winning the match… until Andrew dropped his 11 carp on the scales for 97lb 14oz! I ended up second, and received a nice £50 for my efforts.

With 48lb taking third spot, I was pleased that I hadn't spent too much time looking for a carp, and hindsight tells me that the decisions that I made were sound.

Sadly, I don't get it right all of the time, and you obviously have to be lucky enough to have the fish in front of you in order to catch them, as I did at Lakeside. That said, adopting this 'safe' mentality has been working really well for me lately. As I sit here writing this, I have picked up money in seven out of the last eight matches that I have fished and, even though most of them have only been section prizes, they are a damn sight better than driving home with nothing.

| *You never know what the next fish is going to be with Tom's approach.*

| *Get your feeding right, and winning bags like this will come easy!*

Light Is Right!

The feeding strategy I have described is all about getting bites and keeping fish coming, and I carry this philosophy through to my rig choice too. The fish in our commercial waters are more wary than ever now, and often shy away from thick lines, and big, positive rigs.

Some anglers are scared of fishing too light, in case they hook a big fish, and get snapped. While it is always wise to match your tackle to the size of fish that you are expecting to catch, I also firmly believe that you should fish as light as you feel you can get away with – in my mind there is no doubt whatsoever that doing so gets you more bites.

My float choice on this occasion was a light 4x10 Mick Wilkinson Slim, with 0.11mm Reflo Power main line to a 0.08mm Reflo Power hooklength. I used this in conjunction with a Preston No9 Hollo, and had no problem in landing everything that I hooked.

COMMERCIAL SWIMS EXPLAINED

ISLAND POINT

GETTING IT RIGHT...

Welsh international **Andy Neal** shows you his four-swim approach that rules the roost on commercial fisheries.

SHORT MEAT SWIM

MARGINS

OPEN-WATER SKIMMER SWIM

White Springs Fishery
Pontardulais, Swansea,
Wales SA4 8QG
t: 01792 885699
w: www.whitespringsfishery.co.uk

Andy Neal
Age: 33
Lives: Ebbw Vale
Sponsors: Frenzee, Bait-Tech
Team: None

Many commercial swims are full of luscious features to fish against, and when you combine these with the underwater contours and consideration of margin swims, it's easy to see why anglers can get ravelled up in a confusion of rigs and baits!

Having fished commercials throughout the country, I usually find myself coming back to four basic lines of attack that nearly always bring me a good result.

To demonstrate these, I've brought you to White Springs Fishery near Swansea, a well-developed commercial offering a vast range of challenging options to the matchman!

Swim Assessment

I see far too many anglers dash to their peg, plonk their seatbox down and hastily plumb up a swim with little consideration. I'll often sit for up to 10 minutes, making an assessment of the peg and planning out where my target areas are going to be. Today, I have an island at around 16 metres, with an attractive point to fish towards. These are always fantastic features, as you not only catch the resident fish that swim around the islands, but also pull fish from in open water.

The next area calling out to me is the near bank. Matches nowadays are generously pegged, and you'll often have a spare platform to one side. Resident fish live down the margins, patrolling the near bank throughout the day. I prefer to target just one edge to reduce complication. Today I've got much more cover down the left-hand margin, and I actually need to stand up to see my float. This side is also towards the open water in the gap of two islands, giving me more room to draw fish from. Had I chosen the right-hand margin, I'd have less water to pull fish from because of the narrower gap where the island starts.

I'm then faced with open-water swims. With the bankside disturbance, wiser fish back off into open space and by setting traps in the deepest water you can often catch the odd bonus fish to give you that extra winning weight. Rather than positioning an open-water swim just anywhere, I select a spot that has some kind of underwater feature. Commercials are rarely flat everywhere, and there's normally a near shelf sloping away to deep water. The bottom of this is a great area to target; a natural place for food to gather, and a patrol route for active carp. More often than not, this is on a short length of pole, anything up to six metres from the bank, making it perfect to feed regularly by hand.

The three swims I've already selected are primarily for targeting carp. However, like many commercials, White Springs is stocked with some lovely skimmers, and I'll often have an hour in the middle of the match targeting these when the carp have switched off. I position this swim where I feel the carp don't want to be. Skimmers are fairly delicate fish, and will get well out of the way of the more aggressive species. Fishing a sensible distance of 11 to 13 metres in open water is always a safe bet.

Bait Choices

Five baits cover nearly all my commercial fishing, allowing me to target fish of all sizes on different swims. The first is one that's very instant – pellets. Commercials have these introduced all year round, and carp throughout the country become addicted to them. I find that micros and 4mms suffice for nearly all my pole fishing. I also stick to two sizes of Bait-Tech Expanders for the hook, 4mms and 6mms.

If F1s are the target 4mms are better, while a 6mm avoids the attention of small fish and is much more effective for proper carp. Today, the island point is perfect for targeting with pellets, offering a sensible depth of two feet, where I can confidently feed a mixture of soaked micros and 4mms without worry of foul hooking fish.

Corn is a favourite bait of mine when the weather picks up. Its heavy nature means it stays hard on the bottom, and doesn't waft up when carp are feeding. It also makes an excellent hook bait, and I'll never be seen without it on my side tray. This is my number one choice for feeding down the margins in conjunction with some hard 4mm pellets. Carp can't become preoccupied with these baits, and both are fairly heavy

| *A strong, stable float pattern is favoured for meat.*

| *Another pot-bellied specimen hits the net!*

A mixture of meat and polony is effective.

particles that keep the fish on the bottom. I'll regularly slip a grain of corn on the hook over my long pellet swim too, and even try a piece for skimmers if small fish pose problems.

Next up is meat, a high-oil bait that is great for picking out bigger fish. I like to feed meat on the shorter swim in open water, where I'm looking at priming the line for later in the session. I find myself using 6mm cubed meat, no matter where I'm fishing, and have a great little trick up my sleeve to put me ahead of the competition. It involves mixing two kinds of meat together; the first is simply Bait-Tech Boosted Meat, with the second being N-Tice Polony. This is slightly tougher, much darker in colour and carries a very spicy taste that carp seem to love! These also sink at slightly different rates and create an attractive cascade of cubes in the water column to give maximum fish-attracting potential.

For skimmers, I favour a more traditional groundbait approach. Feeding three balls loaded with dead maggots and some micro pellets ensures that there's always a good bed of bait on the bottom. This means I haven't got to worry about topping up or refeeding the swim, and I can simply drop on this when things are looking quiet to keep putting fish in the net!

My mix is particularly interesting, and comprises of a mixture of Kult Sweet Fishmeal and Big Carp Krill & Tuna Method Mix. These produce a highly potent recipe, which contains all the attractive fishy smells that bream love, with some added sweet smells and breadcrumb. My favourite hook bait for this swim is two dead maggots, although I'll also try a 4mm expander if any small fish pose a problem.

Rigs With Reasons!

I'm not an angler for setting up loads of rigs, but to approach a commercial swim correctly you can't make do with just one rig for many swims.

On my island swim I've got two feet of water, and need a short, slim float that will take plenty of weight.

Heavy baits are fed in the margins.

My choice is a 0.2g Frenzee FM1, incredibly strong, with a medium diameter hollow-plastic bristle. I place my shot in a simple bulk just eight inches from the hook. This prevents my expander pellet hook bait getting wafted away from the feed area where I'm more likely to foul hook fish. This is tied on 0.15mm Vertex main line for durability, with an 0.11mm hook link of the same, and size 16 Tubertini 808 hook.

Elastic is important here, and I opt for pink Stretch Hollow Elastic from Frenzee, the lightest grade in the range. This not only allows me to use the light trace to get more bites, but also means fish will bolt out of the shallow swim with little disturbance.

The margin swim is a little deeper than across, so I've chosen an identical rig but with a 0.3g float, and the next grade up yellow Stretch. I'm likely to encounter slightly bigger fish down the edge, so this will hopefully give me a little more control.

Moving on to the short meat rig, I've set up a longer, more stable FP700 Float, which also incorporates a strong spring-eye design. Shotting for this rig is less positive, as the slow fall of the meet means that carp often intercept the bait as it settles. I opt for a simple bulk just below half depth, with two No9 droppers below. Main line is again 0.15mm, with an 0.135mm hook link and heavier Tubertini 175 hook in a size 16. Elastic is again Pink Stretch Hollow, allowing fish to swim out of the peg with little disturbance.

Things are scaled down when it comes to my skimmer rig. My float is a 0.5g FM6, incorporating a wire stem and thin, hollow-plastic bristle. This is a very stable pattern to help hold the float still, but also slim, offering little resistance when one picks up the bait. I scale down my lines to 0.135mm main line, with an 0.10mm trace, and use a smaller

Andy targets skimmers mid-match.

size 18 Tubertini 808 hook. A bulk 18 inches from the hook, with the same two No9 droppers, completes the rig.

Making It Work

After looking at today's swim, I decide my best opening gambit is going to be the island point. This is a natural fish-holding area, and I expect fish to be here from the off. For this reason, I don't introduce any large amounts of bait, and simply kick off with a small Soft Pot of dampened micros with a few 4mms and the odd grain of corn. My skimmer swim is fed with three balls of the mix, lightly 'nipped' together to ensure they break down quickly. A handful of the mixed cubes go in on the short meat swim, and I also introduce a full pot of corn and 4mms down the margin.

I start the session with a single grain of corn across to the island,

White Springs offers both open water and island options, creating scope for several swims.

Don't be afraid to stand up to see past marginal cover when fishing down the edge.

Andy favours both sweet and fishmeal mixes.

and am a little disappointed when the float doesn't budge! After several minutes of lifting and dropping, I have a quick dip before a spooky carp bolts out of the peg – damn! I quickly ship in, rebait with an expander, and trickle in a few more free offerings. This time things happen a little differently, and just as I'm tapping the last few pellets from the pot, my elastic shoots from the pole tip! After a 'spirited' little battle, a small ghost carp is soon in the net.

Several more fish follow, with a change to a 6mm expander proving to be successful. Things aren't as hectic as expected, which isn't a bad thing, and keeps me on my toes to prime my other swims in a bid to keep fish coming. After every fish from the island, I've been throwing 20 or so 4mm pellets down the margin, along with a few grains of corn. The meat line is also primed on a regular basis, fed with a dozen cubes every few minutes. This is often a good line late in the match, and while many anglers catch down the margins in the last hour, this open-water meat swim can really produce the goods!

I notice some fizzing and bubbles from over my groundbait, which screams out fish. Baiting up with double maggot, I'm confident of a good run of skimmers on this now. The whole of the float bristle popping out of the water signals the first bite, and I'm instantly into a 2lb specimen. An even bigger chap follows on the next drop in, before several smaller samples around the 10oz mark put in an appearance. This short, 20-minute run of fish puts another 12lb in the net, and proves the effectiveness of the swim!

With the final two hours looming, I'm itching to have a go down the margins, and am still priming the short meat swim. I like to feed a few 4mms and some corn in via a Soft Pot, and lower my hook bait straight on top of this to get an instant bite. My theory's proved correct, with five pot-bellied carp in as many drops! I'm now curious as to how good the meat line is going to be, and with an hour remaining it's time to have a look!

First drop-in produces a surprise 3lb bream, which must have been brave as the next six drops all produce carp! It's much better to feed as soon as a fish is hooked here, so the bait is settled on the bottom by the time you next go in. A soft elastic allows you to do this with little worry of where the fish is going. It's working, as I'm suffering few liners, and every bite is an unmissable sharp pull-under!

I have a real hectic last hour, and even start putting fish straight back into the lake as I was pushing the net limit! Well over 80lb of carp, combined with 20lb plus of silvers, proves the importance of targeting the correct swims at certain times. Next time you sit at your peg, have a good think about where and how you're going to fish, and you're sure to win more matches!

Another winning bag of carp and skimmers, all down to careful consideration of where to fish!

frenzee
Bagging by Design

INTRODUCING
Frenzee Soft Pots

THE SOFTEST, SAFEST, MOST UNIVERSAL POLE POT AVAILABLE

- **No more split or damaged pole sections**
- **3 sizes for varying amounts of feed**
- **Sprinkle lids included for drip feeding**
- **Easy to remove**
- **Easy to use**

Simply squeeze the sides of the soft pot to open the cavity bore (the base will open like a clothes peg). It's then a case of simply putting the pot on the pole at the required position and letting go! The two open sides will then close around the tip section, gripping the pole and leaving the pot firmly in place!

EACH PACK COMES COMPLETE WITH A SET OF 3 POTS INCLUDING SPRINKLE LIDS IN SIZES SMALL, MEDIUM & LARGE.

RRP £4.99 PER PACK

"The safest most universal pot available. A simple yet brilliant design that fits where YOU want it to! Made for a reason – THEY WORK!"

Andy Neal

CHECK OUT FRENZEE'S PRODUCT RANGE AT:

WWW.FRENZEE.CO.UK

SALES HOTLINE 01686 622400 OR CONTACT YOUR LOCAL STOCKIST

WINNING BREAM TACTICS

Viaduct Fishery
Cary Valley, Somerton,
Somerset TA11 6LJ
t: 01458 274022
w: www.viaductfishery.com

Lee Werrett
Age: 40
Lives: Ebbw Vale
Sponsors: Middy, Bait-Tech
Team: None

THE ONLY WAY IS UP!

Lee Werrett takes us to Viaduct Fishery, unveiling the secrets behind lift bites for bream!

I love fishing for bream all year round and have found one particular method very effective. It involves fishing for lift bites and where many people suffer problems with liners and missed bites, I've figured out how to get a positive lift indication every time! Last winter I caught over 194lb of silvers in four matches here at Viaduct, and regularly catch in excess of 70lb during summer!

The method is very simple and works anywhere that holds a good head of bream and skimmers. As with any form of fishing, there are two essential things to get right for this method to be effective – feeding and presentation!

Feeding

My usual routine is to feed two areas and rotate between them. This is the key to keeping fish coming for the duration of a match. It's a good idea to try and find the same depth on both swims and position them at angles so that they are several metres apart.

Feeding two swims allows me to introduce different volumes of bait on each, and quickly work out what's best. I also have the option of feeding different kinds of baits in each area, for example, maggots on one and pellets on the other.

Targeting two areas enables you to keep catching for much longer than you would by feeding a single area. I normally feed one swim and let that settle while I fish the other. On a good day you can catch a couple of fish off one swim before topping it up and swapping to the other. It gives the fish time to settle after each top-up, gaining confidence before you drop back in again. It's simple, but really effective, and a great way of keeping the bites coming!

The Rig

My rig is a key part of this method's success and, although it's simple, I've spent a lot of time getting it right. It's what many people refer to as a double-bulk rig. As the name suggests, this involves two blocks of shot. The first is a main bulk, which is typically placed 14 to 18 inches from the hook; far enough off the bottom to avoid these large-flanked fish brushing it. The second 'bulk' consists of two or three smaller shot grouped together just two or three inches from the hook.

Accurate plumbing up is absolutely vital with this rig and you must get the second bulk set just off the bottom. The shotting pattern is brilliant for many other bottom-feeding fish. When they pick the bait up the float will either disappear when the fish dislodges the bulk, or rise up out of the water like a beacon as they lift the bulk off the bottom! Either way, the bites are very positive and can be easily distinguished from liners. This is a really satisfying approach when you get it right; there's nothing better than clunking the hook home into a nodding bream after a positive lift bite!

To help magnify the lift-bite effect, I doctor some pole floats so that they have an extra-long bristle with a sight bob on the end. I use my favourite Middy Carp Grey 1 pattern. This has a bulbous body and stable wire stem, but I replace the bristle with one that's about half an inch longer. The finished float cuts through the surface skim, dots down nicely and lifts up positively when the double bulk is displaced.

I shot my float so that the main bulk takes the float down to the base of the bristle and then the double bulk dots the full bristle down. The second bulk is typically two or three No10s rather than one larger shot, because this gives me a little more flexibility. Sometimes, spacing these shot just 10 millimetres apart can make a big difference to the quality of bites that you get, too.

I'm using a 0.10mm Middy Lo-Viz hooklength but when it gets even warmer I will normally scale up to a minimum of a 0.12mm hooklength, especially when there's a chance of hooking a carp. I prefer 10in hooklengths for the extra stretch that they offer and have no problem putting shot on this trace. I actually use Stotz throughout because they seem to be much kinder to the line.

My elastic is Middy 1-5 through the full top two of my XK55 pole. This is a really light grade, so plenty comes out on the strike. The soft elastic reduces the chances of bumping fish, plus it gives me a better chance of getting any foul-hookers in. The fish also seem to fight less on lighter gear and you can ship back steadily and guide them to

Topping up is vital with bream.

Use the accuracy of a pole pot to maximise your catch!

the net quite easily.

Another good tip with this method is to have a conventional rig set up too, with a bulk and two or three droppers. Sometimes the fish will sit off the bottom rather than feed hard on the deck and this rig will allow me to catch these during quiet spells. The double-bulk rig is ultra-positive and designed to get the bait straight to the bottom, whereas the conventionally shotted rig comes into play when bites are iffier.

Location

Another part of the jigsaw is exactly where to fish. I find it best to fish as far away from you as is comfortable, to put space between you and the bream. This is especially true from winter through to spring, when the water is still quite clear. Having said this, once you get to summer and autumn you can catch really big weights at just five or six metres out! I'm fishing 14.5 metres, a typical distance that I'd look to fish on most venues.

Baits

Double bulking for skimmers will work with practically any bait. A great little trick of mine is to feed pellets in groundbait. Bait-Tech Kult is my favourite for skimmers, which I've darkened off with a sprinkling of black dye. This is a sweet fishmeal mix, full of molasses and perfect for skimmers throughout the year. When targeting big bream, or when expecting a really big weight, I add 50 per cent Special 'G' to increase the fishmeal content even more.

When it comes to the size of top-up balls, I have a rule involving feeding just one-handed balls. Depending on how well it's fishing, I will usually top up with one or two of these after every couple of fish. You should be able to fit a couple of them in a big cupping-kit pot.

This is also the amount of feed that I will normally kick off with. I find that skimmers feed best on commercials with small amounts of bait cupped in regularly.

This feeding pattern works well in conjunction with my two-swim approach; it allows you to quickly gauge what quantities of feed are working best on the day. Some days one top-up ball is ample, while on others two is the way to go. Once you've worked it out, you can commit both swims to the same feeding regime and hopefully bag up!

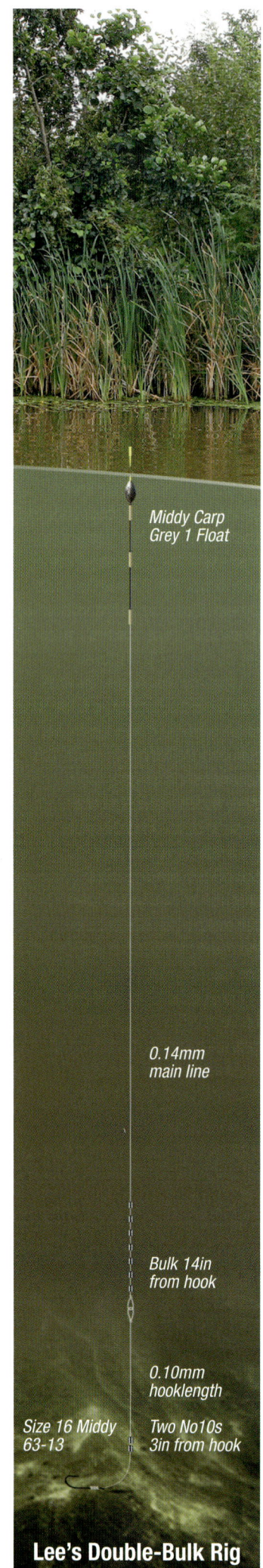

Putting It Into Practice

I'm sat on the back bank of Spring Lake at Viaduct. Fishing at 14.5 metres, I feed one ball containing 50 micro pellets to my right and two balls containing casters to my left, both in Kult groundbait. It's a flat-calm, sunny day with barely a ripple on the lake, far from ideal skimmer conditions! I'm relieved to get my first fish 20 minutes into the session and at just over 1lb it's typical of the stamp of fish that I'm after.

Bites are a little finicky at the start, with very few pronounced 'lifts' in the still conditions. The maggot swim is easily best at this early stage. As the session wears on, however, the pellet swim seems to really kick into life and gradually becomes the most productive bait with a 4mm Xpand pellet on the hook.

After a couple of hours I have about 15lb in the net, coinciding with a slight breeze blowing from right to left. This seems to really help inject some activity and bites suddenly become much more positive, with 80 per cent of them being the unmistakable lifts that I was hoping for!

With the fish feeding really well over the pellet swim, I make the decision to cut out the casters and feed groundbait and pellets on both swims. Two top-up balls containing a pinch of micros in each is really working and I'm able to pick up a couple of good skimmers off each spot in rotation.

I've ended up with a big 40lb-plus bag of skimmers, the biggest nudging 3lb. The swim has become increasingly stronger as the day's progressed and come the end of the session I was getting a positive lift bite every drop-in! Get the rig and feeding right and this is exactly what you can expect. Try it and I guarantee that you will be impressed!

| *Efficient rigs and feeding lead to winning bags like this!*

Lee's Double-Bulk Rig

- Middy Carp Grey 1 Float
- 0.14mm main line
- Bulk 14in from hook
- 0.10mm hooklength
- Size 16 Middy 63-13
- Two No10s 3in from hook

MIDDY MATCH RANGE

NUMBER 1 FOR MATCH ACCESSORIES

↑ Hi-Viz and Lo-Viz: the winning combo. Whether you choose Original Solid Hi-Viz elastic or the new Shock-Core Hollow you can be sure that, used with Lo-Viz line, you have the best set-up possible.

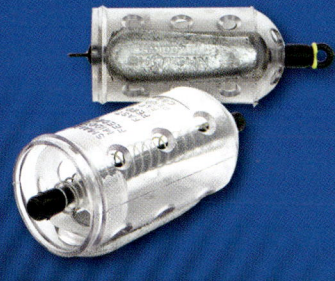

↗ Shot-Gun Pellet Feeders are winning more matches than any other pellet feeder.

↗ 63-13 and 93-13: Teflon impregnated hooks for carp commercials.

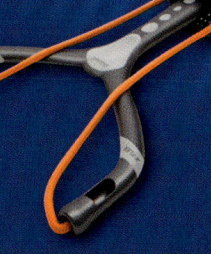

↗ X-Flex Pellet Catapult for pin point accuracy.

↗ Baggin Machine Wagglers: The best up-in-the-water fishing floats in the UK.

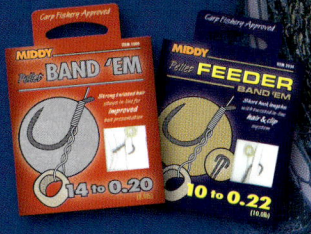

↗ XX55 Pole Floats: Hand made from AA grade balsa and incorporating steel core anti-snag side eyes.

↗ Band 'Em hooks-to-nylon: KM2 hooks tied to Lo-Viz line with a latex band on the hair.

FORGET ABOUT CARP

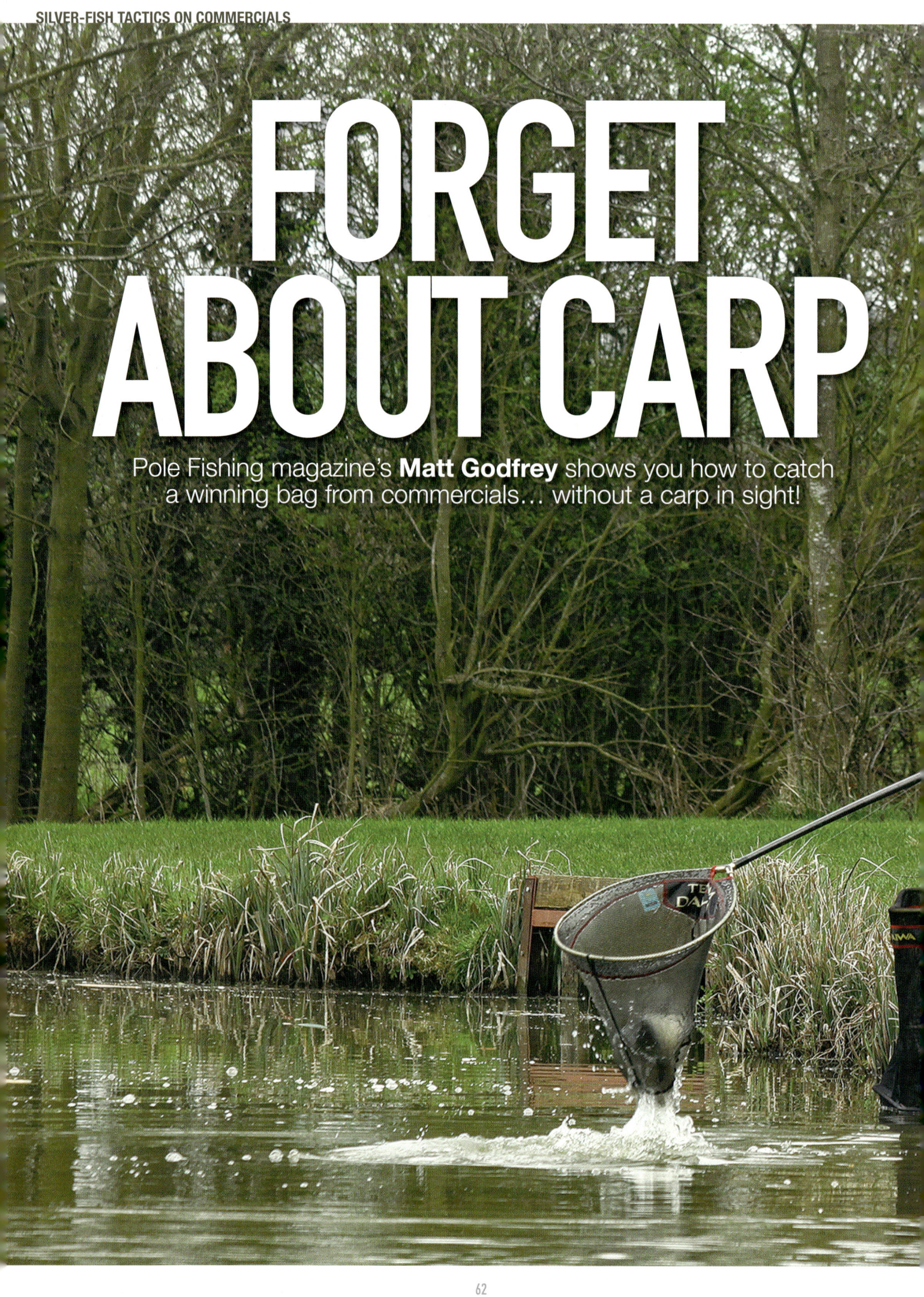

Pole Fishing magazine's **Matt Godfrey** shows you how to catch a winning bag from commercials… without a carp in sight!

Dynamite Baits
Makins Fishery
Near Wolvey, Warwickshire
CV11 6QJ
t: 01455 220877
w: www.makinsfishery.co.uk

Matt Godfrey
Age: 22
Lives: Daventry
Sponsors: None
Team: Ultimate Barnsley Blacks

Many of today's commercial fisheries have developed a stigma whereby if you're not on a certain few carp pegs, you'll struggle to compete. Although anglers will often target and undoubtedly catch some carp on average swims or worse, they will often fall just short of the frame, beaten by a handful of better carp pegs. A major learning point for me over the past 12 months has involved catching silver fish from such areas and, on many occasions, I've beaten the better carp pegs by doing this!

Commercials are full of all kinds of other species, from big roach, rudd and bream to things like tench, hybrids and crucians. These are really chunky fish, and ignored week after week by anglers who simply target carp. Some days, when a lower winning weight is needed, you can catch enough silvers to win the match. On other days, a great tactic is to target carp for the first and last hours when they're most willing to feed, and catch a weight of silvers in the middle hours.

| *Double No3 Slip elastic is perfect for commercial silvers.*

| *Feeding finely minced worms helps hold fish in the peg for long periods.*

You'll be surprised as to the weight that can be amassed and, more often than not, an odd carp will muscle in on the action. Let me tell you more about my simple but effective approach…

Baits

There are two bait combinations I consider when targeting commercial silvers. Casters and worms are without a doubt my number one choice. These catch a diverse range of fish all year round, and are very versatile as to how and where they can be fished.

Chopped worm is one of the best baits to attract and hold fish, while casters always pick out the better samples. They can be loose fed to catch shallow, and constantly draw in more and more fish. The great thing about my approach is that you don't need a big, expensive bait list. Just a quarter of a kilo of worms and two pints of casters are more than ample for a match.

Even in the cooler months, I prefer to fish worms and casters as opposed to maggots, simply because of the quality fish these baits attract. Everything will muscle its way in with worms and casters. Maggots have a tendency to bring in lots of small fish, which can be particularly frustrating, and you'll often need a lot more bait to try to feed them off!

My other bait choices for commercial silvers are pellets. With so much fishmeal going into fisheries, their heads of silvers have inevitably developed a taste for them. However, rather than going all guns blazing with a big-pellet carp approach, I like to scale everything down to maximise the attraction to species such as bream, tench and crucians.

A great little trick I've learnt is to feed a mixture of 1mm and 3mm pellets. The 1mms are incredibly fine and act as groundbait, allowing fish to graze for long periods, while the 3mms stop them becoming pre-occupied. It's important to give the pellets a good soak so they're soft throughout, also allowing them to be squeezed into small balls to get to the bottom in deep water.

Another little trick of mine involves a little additive too. I've never particularly been one for adding smelly things to bait, but I can confirm this particular one works very well! It comes from Mainline Baits and is the Cell Stick Mix, a very sweet coconut base that takes away any strong fishmeal edge from the pellets. Strangely, this is a carp additive, but I've caught my best nets of commercial skimmers and bream using it.

Where To Fish

Choosing the right swims to target commercial silvers is important. If you're going to look for an early carp or two, I'd advise you plumb up these swims first, and look to keep the silver fish areas well away. As a general rule, I always look to fish worms and casters short, making it very efficient for catching the smaller fish and allowing me to feed by hand. This is vital to keep a stream of loose feed falling through the water. Just five or six sections of pole are usually perfect for this. Always try and find a 'nice' area to target, towards the bottom of the first shelf. By coming slightly out of the full depth, you'll be fishing on a harder bottom away from any silt.

Matt uses as light a float as possible with casters.

Another great little tip is to fish at an angle away from you, which means you won't be dragging fish from any longer swims, or more importantly playing any carp on top of the swim. My usual gambit with pellets is to fish further out in open water. Fish like bream tend to favour such areas, and I simply have a plumb around and find a sensible flat area to fish away from any islands in open water. Distance obviously depends on wind, but 13 metres is usually a sensible starting point.

Feeding

As always, feeding plays a massive role in being successful on commercial silvers. Starting with the shorter swim, I like to kick off with a simple mixture of chopped worms and casters, mixed 50/50. Around a third of a large pole pot is my typical amount, although if things are expected to be difficult, I'll feed a globule the size of a walnut!

One of my little tricks with this is to mince the worms extremely fine. When you think that they're like soup, chop them some more! This means there are thousands of tiny worm shavings on the bottom and suspended in the water column, holding fish in the area for really long periods. I then regularly loose feed casters over the top, and vary the amounts depending on how the session is going. On some days, the bigger fish will be really cagey, and give you the tiniest of bites. You can often tell when the fish are not confident if they are hooked right on the edge of the mouth. Feeding just a dozen casters every time you lay in the rig is really effective in creating competition.

On other days, there'll be a lot of small fish in the peg, and you'll need to feed larger amounts, but less regularly, to pin the bigger fish down. If you do experience lean spells or feel the peg is dying, another effective trick is to re-feed with a small pinch of the really finely chopped worms. This seems to get the fish buzzing around again.

The pellet swim requires a different feeding approach, and I'll

| *Try to guide any big fish out of the swim to prevent feeding fish becoming spooked.*

usually introduce pellets at three or four intervals in the first hour. Just enough pellets to cover the bottom of a large pole-pot is about right, sprinkled in over an area of a few square feet to allow numerous fish to graze over them. Doing this several times allows spooky fish like bream to gain confidence, and you'll often experience a good initial run of fish when you first go on this swim.

A small pole-mounted pot is the perfect way of feeding when you go on this swim. Always line up with a far-bank marker when feeding like this, to allow the hook bait to be placed right on top of a small concentration of feed. The wider scatter of bait created by the initial feed with a larger pole pot keeps fish grazing once one is hooked.

Rigs

Getting your rigs right is important when targeting commercial silvers. The biggest area

Who wouldn't be happy catching fish like this?

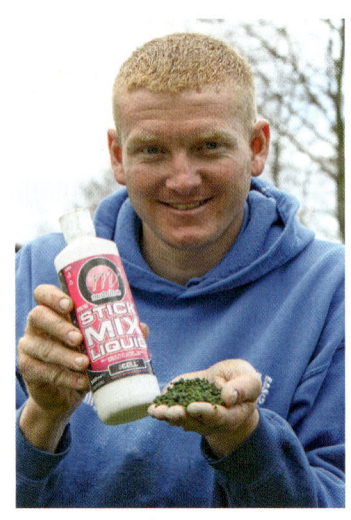

Shhh… Matt's secret additive!

where people slip up, in my opinion, is fishing too heavy with regard to lines and hooks. My natural-water experience has definitely taught me that fishing light gets you more bites from the bigger, more wary fish.

Starting with the caster rig, my float choice is a Preston Chianti, a slim pattern with a cane bristle. Main line is 0.11mm Reflo Power, to a 21cm hooklength of 0.08mm. My favourite hook is a size 16 Gamakatsu Gama Black – small enough to bury in a caster, but big enough to hold a worm head or double bait. When I'm really bagging, or if some big fish arrive, I'll step up to an 0.10mm trace and size 16 Tubertini 808 hook. Elastic is important, and must be light enough so the fish don't splash on the surface, but heavy enough to cope with swinging chunky fish and taming the odd bonus. After much experimentation, I've settled on a doubled No3 Preston Slip elastic, which works an absolute treat.

My shotting pattern is nearly always a tapered spread of No11s, starting close together at half depth, before getting further apart moving towards the hook. I always aim to use as light a float as possible given the conditions and depth. As a general guide, I'll use a 3x8 size in three feet of water or less, a 4x10 in depths to five feet, and a 4x12 for anything more. This sounds light, but definitely sorts out the bigger fish, and you'll also see and hit many more bites with a light float.

For pellets my rig is different again, as I'm aiming to hold a pellet static for bigger fish. I opt for my favourite Mick Wilkinson Pinger float, incorporating a longish wire stem, round body and highly visible, but still sensitive, plastic bristle. Main line is again 0.11mm, with a shorter 15cm hook link of 0.10mm, and size 16 Tubertini 808 hook.

To make this rig as sensitive as possible, I've found a strung bulk of No11s an inch apart, starting just above the hook link, is about right. This is basically an F1 rig, with the feeding tailored more for skimmers. Elastic is yellow MAP Hollow in conjunction with a puller kit. This is soft throughout, with loads of stretch if a carp is hooked. I've found it's hard to get broken with this gear, and have landed fish well into double figures by taking things easy.

Putting It Into Practice!

To demonstrate the effectiveness of my simple approach for commercial silvers, I've brought you to Reptile Pool at the famous Dynamite Baits Makins Complex. This is a typical venue where targeting silvers can be massively effective, and there are some really impressive fish to catch by doing it. For the purposes of the feature, I'm not even considering carp today.

I'm feeding my worm-and-caster line just up the near shelf at six sections, with a pellet swim in open water at 13 metres. After feeding the initial bait, I begin by feeding a dozen casters regularly on the short line, and connect with quality fish from the off. First drop-in produces a 10oz hybrid, and I manage several big roach and some gritty old Makins perch in the first 40 minutes!

However, the regular feeding seems to have brought in a mass of small rudd, so I start feeding a big pouch of casters every few minutes to pin the bigger fish down. It certainly works, with a 3lb bream, two tench and a run of crucians coming to the net, most falling to a double caster hook bait. I've been potting some pellets on the longer swim, although I'm reluctant to try it with such good sport on the caster swim!

With the odd bubble appearing, I decide to have a go. First drop with a 4mm expander soon leads to yards of elastic coming from the pole, with an angry 6lb ghost carp on the end! It's soon subdued on the light gear, and would be a welcome bonus in a match! Things are quiet for a few minutes after the disturbance, but after several introductions of bait with the pole-mounted pot, it isn't long before I'm into a skimmer.

Another follows, with several bigger bream, before a common carp decides to jump on the stage! Throughout the day I alternate between the pellet and caster swims, feeding a decent amount of bait on each swim before resting it. Casters provide the bread-and-butter fish, with roach to 10oz, and the odd bonus. Pellets also prove successful, with five bream, several tench and some skimmers hitting the net, not discounting the brace of greedy carp! Three and half hours into the session, the silver-fish net is looking rather full, so we decide to get the catch shot and carry on enjoying the sport.

Over 70lb of quality commercial silvers make for an excellent morning's sport. Next time you draw a less than average carp peg, make it a winner by taking advantage of the fish many anglers ignore!

A real mixed bag from a commercial – enough to win without carp!

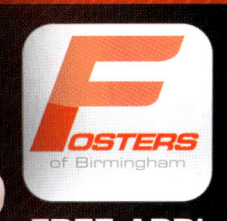

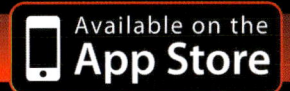

THE EXPERTS' ANGLE

MATT HALL

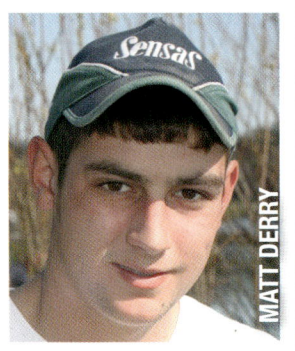

MATT DERRY

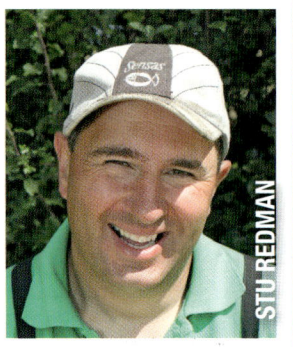

STU REDMAN

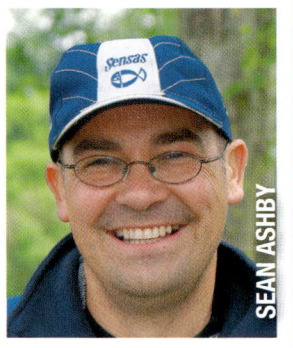

SEAN ASHBY

ROB HEWISON

DARRAN BICKERTON

JOE ROBERTS

MIXED-BAG MAGIC!

Sensas' team of experts bring you eight top tips to help you win more silver-fish matches

Get Muddy!
with Stu Redman

Mud, mud, glorious mud; there's nothing quite like it for catching rudd… and tench, chub, roach, perch, bream – you name it! Anglers have been taking advantage of soils and leams for countless years on canals, rivers and natural stillwaters. It's a great way of adding a much-needed cloud to the water so that the fish feel safer as they feed.

You can also use them to great success on commercial fisheries. Soil and leams are great bulking agents when mixed with other groundbaits, and a way of getting your bait exactly where you want it. Soil can actually be dyed by adding Sensas Tracix and Carp Colour powdered dyes. A small amount will visibly change the shade of the soil, but it is only when it touches the water that you'll see its clouding properties to the full.

Yellow dye makes the longest-lasting cloud, ideal for small fish. Red is great in conjunction with red baits like maggots and chopped worms. Black is also a favourite, perfect in clearer conditions to make the soil even darker, which helps keep a suspension of colour in the water.

| *Adding dyes and flavours to soils and leams can be very effective.*

| *Soil and leam contain zero feed content, but still offer lots of attraction.*

Work The Flow
with Darran Bickerton

The key to maximising your chances of catching wary fish on moving water is to make your hook bait look as natural as possible. Setting up a number of different rigs allows you to really vary your presentation through the course of a session.

An important thing to bear in mind is that you should never be too confident that the rig you are fishing with is the right one. On some rock-hard days, when you would think a really light rig would be the only way that you can get a bite, a very heavy rig that bombs bait down to the bottom can be best. Likewise, when you are getting a fish every drop-in on a heavy rig and believe

A spray bar helps slow down a rig.

| *Chub love a cloud!*

Use different floats to vary presentation, particularly in moving water.

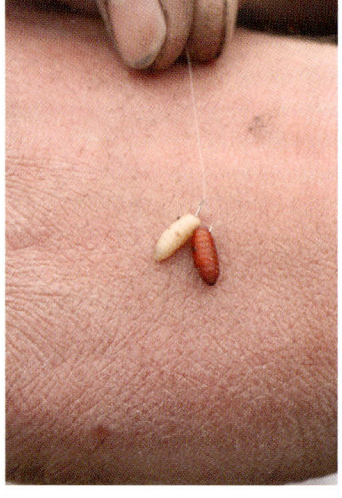

One light and one dark – deadly!

Be positive to catch big canal fish!

Bonus perch like this will regularly fall to a juicy half-worm hook bait.

there is no advantage to fishing a lighter one, trying it can often see your stamp of fish increase!

To hold a bait still you have two options with float choice: you can either set up a large round-bodied float or a smaller flat float. The lighter the float you can get away with while still holding the bait still the better, because then the fish will feel less resistance when it takes the bait.

The Sensas Nautilus is a great float on moving water, due to its versatility. It can be used for either inching a bait through the swim at around half the pace of the current, or running through at the same rate as the flow. They are surprisingly effective and one of the most versatile flowing-water patterns on the market, despite their strange shape. I've had some of my best river sessions using them!

Catching Canal Critters
with Matt Derry

Many of our canals are full of real gritty bonus fish – those rugged bream and battle-scarred stripeys are all big fish well worth targeting in matches! Such fish require a positive approach, and the most consistent bait combo is without a doubt chopped worms and casters. Positioning a swim down the central track at an angle away from you is always a good trick, allowing the better fish to settle away from bankside disturbance. Bream often live in the deepest water and by fishing just at the bottom of the far shelf you can intercept any fish patrolling the shelves and main track.

Always feed plenty of bait for big fish; kicking off the swim with a good handful of chopped worms, with the same amount of casters, is a sensible option. Another great tip is to be conscious of time spent on this swim. Long periods sitting and waiting on it are no good, and if there's a big fish present it will usually pick up the bait in a matter of minutes.

After the initial feed, it's a good idea to loose feed the odd caster over the top of this swim. This creates noise and keeps bait falling through the layers to attract fish into the peg. If nothing shows after initially trying here, don't hesitate to re-feed with another decent amount of bait. You have nothing to lose by doing this and a big fish could have easily been and mopped the lot up while you've been fishing elsewhere!

Big hook baits are also important here. Half a worm is a very versatile and effective option, as is double caster. A great little trick on canals is to hook one very light-coloured caster, and one very dark one. This has been a secret combo for many canal anglers over the years.

Worm Bomb!
with Joe Roberts

Fishing chopped worm and groundbait is one of the most satisfying and easy methods around, and catches everything that swims. It also catches the right sort of fish – namely bream and skimmers, plus quality roach, tench, perch and crucians.

A great little trick that works on both natural and commercial venues is to feed a worm mixture in groundbait. This keeps fish searching for bait, and stops them munching all your feed in one go, hopefully holding them in the peg for a full match. You don't need tons of bait to be successful with chopped worm, and just two handfuls of wrigglers are more than enough for a match. This can be bulked out with other baits such as dead red maggots and casters, which can also be minced up with the worms to release further juices and floating shells.

It's worth keeping the choppy mix of worms, maggots and casters in a separate tub, and only adding it to groundbait just before feeding.

Groundbait is the key to this method's success. Sensas Sweet Fishmeal Lake combines the best properties of a traditional, sweet mix with richer fishmeal. Fishmeal has become a staple part of a fish's diet on today's commercials – even roach. When looking to catch a mixed bag with worms and casters, this is a fantastic mix.

A great little trick is to place a good dollop of choppy mix on top of the groundbait. Then cover this with more groundbait before sliding a hand underneath it and cupping the other hand over the top. Lifting out this cupped handful of bait and squeezing together creates a ball of groundbait with a centre packed with goodies – the perfect chopped-worm time bomb! It's like a Kinder Surprise, and you'll have all kinds of

The Worm Bomb!

01 Chop the worms…

02 … along with some dead reds…

03 … and add the shells!

04 A sweet fishmeal mix is best.

05 Place the choppy mix in the groundbait…

06 … and form a ball with the goodies in the middle!

fish trying to get at the feed inside the ball of groundbait!

Whiskered Friends!
with Rob Hewison

Barbel are a species that have become particularly popular in commercials, and can often be targeted on matches with great success. However, these fish can be strange feeders, and favour a nice hard bottom. This is normally found down the edge on commercials, where silt hasn't settled.

They also favour a good depth of three feet, so if you can find this next to any marginal features such as boards, rushes or a spare platform, you're definitely onto a winner!

When the water temperature is high, the barbel become really active, but will often take their time to settle in a swim. When looking to catch them, it's worth priming a swim for at least an hour before even trying it. Having another area to fish is a good option here, so that you can keep having a look without wasting too much time. Once the barbel arrive,

| *You need durable gear for barbel – they have sharp fins and fight very hard!*

| *Barbel love meat and maggots.*

you'll know about it!

Green Sensas Crazy Hollow elastic is ideal for barbel, initially soft for them to swim away from the shoal but soon powering up, allowing you to get their heads up at the netting stages. Rigs must be fairly strong and durable for this hard-fighting species, as their sharp fins and rough skin will rub against the line. At least 0.16mm main line should be used, allowing sensible hook links of 0.14mm. Sensas Classic Power is a fairly new line that is exceptionally strong and abrasion resistant, ideal for barbel work.

Barbel often head for snags or try

Many commercial matches are now won with barbel!

and get under your keepnets, and a have a sharp dorsal-fin hook that can catch on the line. Hemp is a favourite feed bait for barbel – they absolutely love it! Two other baits to fish in conjunction with this are luncheon meat and red maggots. Feeding is very important and it's a good option to cup all the bait down the edge very quietly. The thinking behind this is quite straightforward – you don't want to attract carp or surface-feeding silver fish that could become a nuisance when trying to target the weight-building barbel!

Positively Slim
with Matt Hall

The use of slim floats is something that can be a massive advantage in your fishing. Slim floats are becoming increasingly popular in the UK, and were initially developed on the canals when fishing for lots of small fish. Round-bodied patterns can lead to many missed bites from small fish, as they feel a lot of resistance from the bulbous, round body.

The French are experts on catching lots of small fish, and use a lot of slim patterns. Another advantage of a slim float is that it comes cleanly out of the water on the strike, in turn leading to more

Slim floats offer minimal resistance when a fish takes the bait.

Be positive with shotting!

hooked fish. Two favourite small-fish patterns are the Sensas Auchy and the SA2, a pattern designed by 2012 World Champion Sean Ashby. Many anglers pay little attention to the shape of floats, but when looking to catch large numbers of small fish they're a massive aid!

Another factor that can be combined with using slim floats is positive shotting. Being confident in using heavy floats, with bulks or olivettes close to the hook, will really speed up your fishing. It's very surprising how many extra fish a heavier rig can catch you over a whole match, and in conjunction with a slim float your efficiency will double!

If you can catch five extra fish an hour by using a heavier-bulked rig, you'll catch 25 extra fish over a whole match. Even at just 1oz apiece that's an extra 1lb 9oz! Bulked-down rigs and slim floats are also great for lowering in accurately, allowing you to confidently place your hook bait right over the feed. This often means you get a bite much quicker.

Rules For Redfins
with Sean Ashby

Big roach are extremely wise fish. One of the best ways to trick them into taking a hook bait is to use as light a float as possible given the conditions, but on many open-water venues surface skim and tow can be a problem.

Don't be afraid of setting up three or four sizes of float for the same swim, allowing you to use the lightest one possible as conditions change. It's not unusual for the wind to pick up halfway through a match, or completely drop! If you only have one setup, you'll not be able to fool the biggest redfins!

A fantastic all-round roach float for both commercials and natural venues is the Sensas Series 13. The carbon stem of this float means that the float is always in touch with the shot, and will follow them through the water perfectly. This is important for roach, as they will often intercept the bait on the drop, giving the tiniest of indications. A wire-stemmed pattern would already be cocked, and lead to missed bites.

Using a fairly thin main line is important for roach, something along the lines of 0.12mm. This sinks slower than light lines due to increased drag in the water, and produces an enticing fall. On the opposite end of the scale, light hooklengths are essential for tricking clever, big roach. Scaling down to 0.07mm traces is a great way to trick them, in conjunction with a very fine-wire hook such as a Sensas 3260.

Another great tip to singling out the bigger roach is to concentrate on fishing the bottom third of the water column, and tailor your feeding to congregate the fish in this area. An effective rig for doing this would consist of a small bulk just below half depth, with three No10 droppers below. The bulk takes the bait instantly into the catching zone, while the droppers offer a slow fall through the important last few feet. When you do get a bite, it's usually a positive pull-under as the fish moves the bulk, exaggerating the small indications that big roach often fool us with!

A cracking net of redfins!

Scale down your lines, and take your time with quality silvers.

Matt can put a lot of his success down to using slim floats.

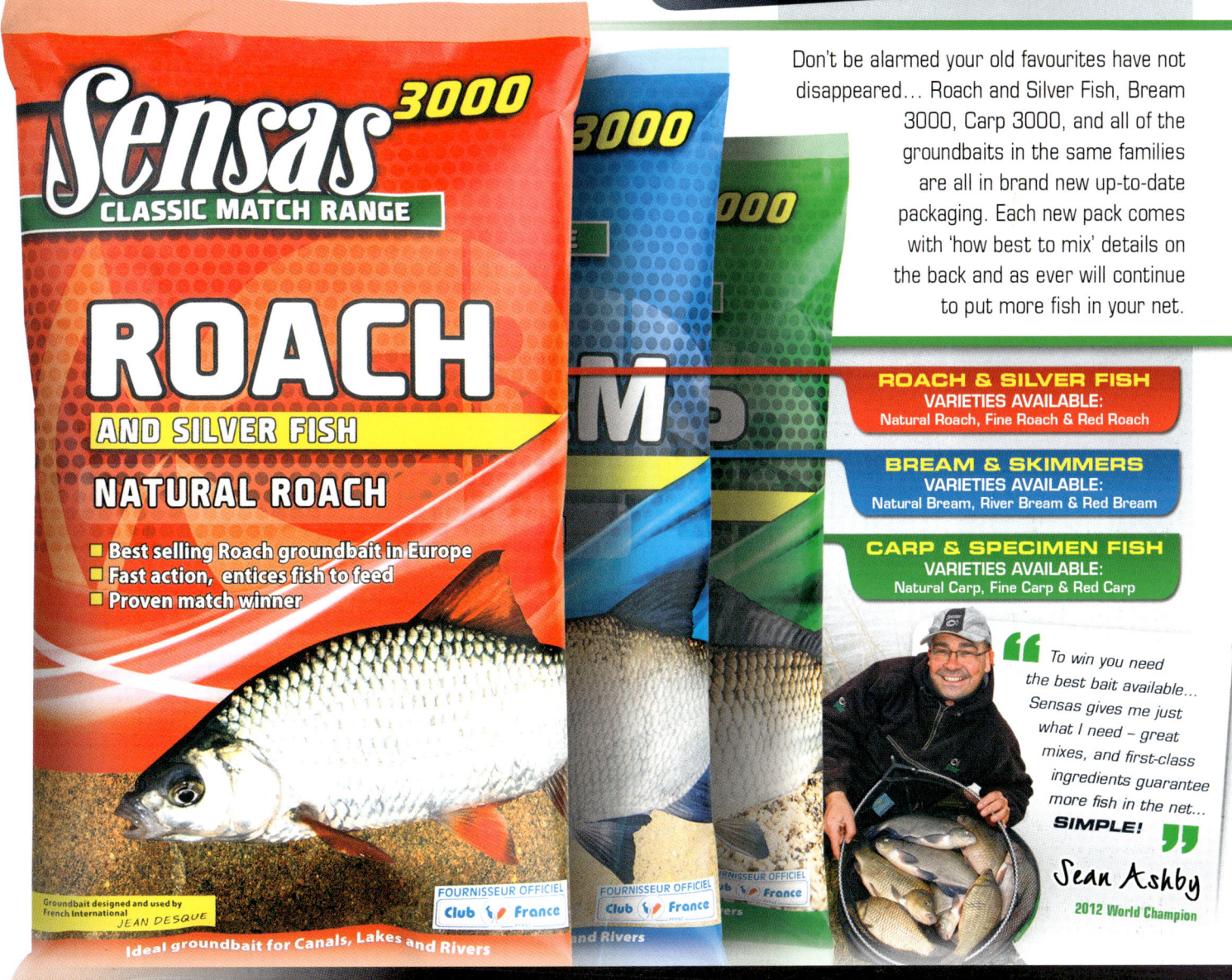

NEW INTRODUCING THE NEW-LOOK

Sensas 3000
CLASSIC RANGE

Don't be alarmed your old favourites have not disappeared... Roach and Silver Fish, Bream 3000, Carp 3000, and all of the groundbaits in the same families are all in brand new up-to-date packaging. Each new pack comes with 'how best to mix' details on the back and as ever will continue to put more fish in your net.

ROACH & SILVER FISH
VARIETIES AVAILABLE:
Natural Roach, Fine Roach & Red Roach

BREAM & SKIMMERS
VARIETIES AVAILABLE:
Natural Bream, River Bream & Red Bream

CARP & SPECIMEN FISH
VARIETIES AVAILABLE:
Natural Carp, Fine Carp & Red Carp

"To win you need the best bait available... Sensas gives me just what I need – great mixes, and first-class ingredients guarantee more fish in the net... SIMPLE!"

Sean Ashby
2012 World Champion

Sensas 3000 Classic Match Range – Roach and Silver Fish – Natural Roach
- Best selling Roach groundbait in Europe
- Fast action, entices fish to feed
- Proven match winner

Groundbait designed and used by French International JEAN DESQUE
Ideal groundbait for Canals, Lakes and Rivers
FOURNISSEUR OFFICIEL Club France

SAME FANTASTIC GROUNDBAITS – GREAT NEW PACKAGING

| FINE ROACH | RED ROACH | RED BREAM | RIVER BREAM | RED CARP | FINE CARP |

5-time world champion Alan Scotthorne has joined the Sensas squad as a bait consultant. Alan has for many years benefited from Sensas's great groundbaits, he has 5 world titles to prove it! Sensas is Team England's sole groundbait supplier.

For more information on the new-look Sensas 3000 Classic Groundbait Range and to check out everything Sensas has to offer, visit our website:

WWW.SENSASMATCH.COM

Sensas

USE BIG BAITS TO YOUR ADVANTAGE

Les Thompson
Age: 35
Lives: Dudley
Sponsors: Matrix, Bait-Tech
Team: Maver Midlands

Wassell Grove Fisheries
Hagley, Worcestershire, DY9 9JH
t: 07967 556673
w: www.wassellgrovefisheries.co.uk

Big baits equal big fish.

THE BIGGER THE BETTER!

Why are double baits better? We join commercial ace **Les Thompson** to find out.

In my eyes, fishing a double hook bait holds a number of key advantages. Most of our commercial fisheries are stuffed with small fish and the areas where we fish for carp, such as the margins and up to islands, often prove popular feeding areas for these as well as their bigger cousins. Often, these are so ravenous that they will intercept a small, single hook bait before a bigger fish has the time to look at it. By fishing two pieces of bait you give yourself the best chance of picking out a big fish from those present in your peg. Also, if you have to sit and wait you can rest safe in the knowledge that if a big fish should come into your peg it will often pick out your hook bait first.

Even in the opposite scenario, when you have a lot of big fish in your peg, I still firmly believe that a big hook bait is better. When fish are feeding confidently, they feed by slurping in the particles off the bottom, and they are bound to find a bigger particle before a smaller one.

A further advantage here is that double hook baits tend to be heavier, so they hold the bottom well. This is a big advantage when, for example, fishing halfway up, or on the top of a slope. When big fish are feeding in your peg, it is not uncommon for the movement of their fins and tails to waft bait down the slope. You can often see this happening to your hook bait because your float moves away from the bank. Not only does this make your hook bait behave unnaturally, but it also means that you have an increased likelihood of seeing false indications and foul hooking fish.

Laying The Carpet

To really get the best from big, double hook baits they should be fished over a carpet of smaller offerings. You have a number of options here, and which bait you choose to use should largely depend on the depth of water that you are fishing in. In shallow water, groundbait is a popular choice. On its day, it can be a deadly carpet, but it also has its minus points. Sometimes the fish become preoccupied with it, meaning they won't accept any other offerings – such as your hook bait!

| *Use a thick bristle with big baits.*

| *Switching to big baits proved the downfall of this "kipper"!*

Pellets can make a very good carpet, although I prefer 4mm and 6mm pellets rather than any smaller offerings. Micro pellets are a deadly carpet bait, too, but again they can lead to fish becoming preoccupied as well as foul-hooked fish.

In water deeper than three feet, hemp and sweetcorn are very effective feed items because they are heavy and don't tend to waft up off the bottom. Obviously, experimenting is key when it comes to deciding which feed to use on a given session because every venue is different. There is nothing to stop you laying three or four carpets in different areas of your peg for the purposes of experimentation.

The Session

I am on the Match Lake at Wassell Grove near Stourbridge, a venue that I have fished a lot over the years. This is a perfect example of a lake where double baits work extremely well because it is full of carp, but also solid with silver fish, which can be a real problem when using single hook baits.

There are plenty of fish of all sizes moving about and to cover my options I'm going to fish three lines – one across to an island at 16 metres, one down the edge up to the pallet to my right, and one on a short-pole line at five metres.

I will feed my edge and short-pole swims by laying down a bed of feed as outlined above, with 4mm pellets being my choice. I will still fish double baits across to the island but because I expect there to be a lot of fish in this area anyway, I will adopt a different feeding strategy. Here I will simply feed a few samples of what I'm planning to fish on the hook via a Toss-Pot, gauging the response before deciding how to proceed.

I'm a big believer in being positive with rigs – after all, you are fishing a big bait on the hook and targeting big fish. My rigs are on 0.16mm line with a 0.14mm hooklength and one of the new Matrix Carp Bagger hooks in a size 14.

There are several rush beds for angry carp to head for so I'm using red Matrix hollow elastic, which is rated as a size 14. I am using a Matrix Series 7 on my short-pole line, and for the shallower water across and down the margins I prefer a Series 1 or Series 3. Each is extremely resilient and can stand up to being dragged through any obstructions.

Past experience has taught me that double meat is the best hook bait on here, although I have also bought other options in the shape of corn, big expander pellets and worms.

I started the session by fishing across to the island, and even though the fish showed signs of spawning, it certainly wasn't affecting their appetite! By Toss-Potting half a dozen pieces of 6mm meat and fishing two pieces on the hook, a procession of small carp came to the net. Out of curiosity, I slipped a single piece on the hook – and promptly caught a gudgeon! I am sure that if I had persevered with it then I would have caught a carp eventually, but fishing double meat was catching me a quality fish a chuck.

The short pole was less productive but, as expected, when I moved down the edge the stamp of fish increased still further. Ambusher!

This method deliberately targets big fish, which are naturally the wisest residents in a venue. When fishing down the edge, a good way of fooling these crafty creatures is to hide your pole tip above any bankside cover that you may have. I have fished up to the adjacent pallet and by fishing a longish line between pole tip and float, I can hide my pole over the pallet so that it is completely hidden from the fish!

I start by introducing a pot full of bait here to create a big bed, but found topping up with a medium Toss-Pot to be the most effective way of keeping fish coming. Again I tried a single hooker and small fish were my only reward. I am convinced that in venues with a prolific mixed head of fish, the bigger the bait that you can present, the bigger the fish you'll catch.

After just three hours' fishing, I pulled my net out to reveal well over 60lb of carp, along with a handful of small fish taken on single hook baits. Point proved!

| Gudgeon can be a nightmare on small baits.

| A selection of baits is required.

| When getting pestered by small fish, try using Les' double-hook-bait tricks!

FRESH::THINKING

MAKE THE CHANGE
...IN SECONDS

MATRIX EVOLUTION
Change from a Method Feeder to a Pellet feeder, or to a straight lead, in seconds without having to break down your kit.

Evolution Method Feeder Open

Evolution Method Feeder Hooped

Evolution Pellet Feeder

Quick Change Lead Clip

Rubber Quick Bead

EVOLUTION

The Matrix Evolution System is a brilliant, simple way of instantly changing from fishing any kind of Evolution feeder to a lead without having to break down your kit.

The secret to the speed is the line slit in the Feeder stem and the Lead Clip. This enables you to position the line through the stem without having to thread it.

Using the Evolution System gives you total flexibility and speed.

From Method Feeder to Pellet Feeder, or to a straight lead in seconds. Just slide the Tail Rubber up, change the feeder or clip and push the Tail Rubber down.

Matrix Evolution Pellet Feeder

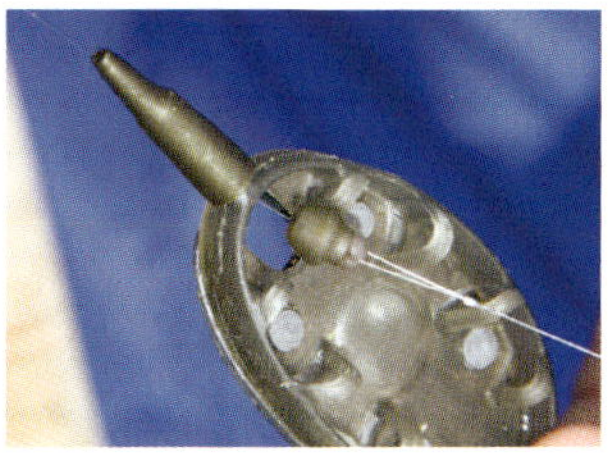

Matrix Evolution Method Feeder

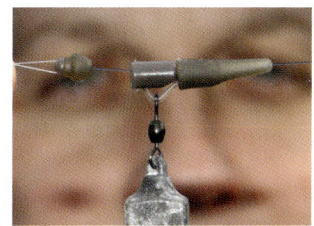

Matrix Evolution Quick Change Lead Clips

NEW NEW NEW NEW NEW NEW

MATRIX®
www.fishmatrix.co.uk

http://www.facebook.com/FishMatrix

COMMERCIAL WAGGLER AND FEEDER TACTICS

TWO-ROD WARRIOR

Jamie Masson reveals his deadly commercial approach, without a pole in sight!

Jamie Masson
Age: 41
Lives: Rotherham
Sponsors: Maver, Marukyu
Team: Ultimate Barnsley Blacks

Little John Lakes
Ollerton, near Mansfield
NG22 9RG
t: 07715 096738

Five Two-Rod Tips!

1 – Regular Casting
Noise and bait both attract carp. Even during quiet spells, make sure you keep casting to create noise and keep bait going in.

2 – Re-clip
If things are slow, don't be afraid to start a new swim to the left or right. Sometimes the fish have moved just a few feet away.

3 – Vary The Load
Try putting different amounts of pellets on the Method. Sometimes a heavy or lightly loaded Method triggers a better response!

4 – No Rest
Try not to use a rest when fishing the waggler. This keeps you active with casting and allows you to react to bites faster!

5 – Leave It Still
After casting, it pays to leave the waggler or feeder where it's landed. Fish home in on the initial plop and intercept the bait!

Many commercial fisheries have features just beyond pole reach. These may be islands, a far bank, or underwater obstacles. The fact is, they all hold fish, and when other anglers start to pick up their poles, I'm left with the features all to myself!

Bold Approach

You join me at Nottinghamshire's Little John Lakes. This is a typical commercial, with a series of islands at around 20 metres. The majority of anglers who compete here start by fishing a small feeder to the island but are quick to be tempted onto the pole when anglers begin to catch. I've had a great deal of success by targeting the island with a positive two-rod approach, using just the waggler and Method feeder, and leaving my pole in the bag! I concentrate my efforts on a single swim and regularly come out on top by switching between these two rod-and-line tactics!

Simple And Positive

I'm a big believer in fishing to win and always keep things very simple and positive. Pellets are a fantastic bait all year round and I pin a lot of faith in them when targeting carp. I always fish with softened micro pellets around the Method and believe that it's important to have particles on the bottom all the time. Groundbait is great for attracting fish but the fine particles simply aren't positive enough for my liking on the Method!

To prepare my pellets, I soak them for a minute before draining and leaving them to stand. Just before starting the session, a good dousing of Ovaltine helps bind them together, ensuring they stay firmly on the Method for casting but break down quickly in the water.

Method Tackle

I use a small, 25g Drennan inline Method feeder. This may seem heavy for casting the short 20m distance but there are several reasons for my choice. Firstly, you can be much more accurate when casting a heavy feeder, compared with a light one. It also holds the bottom well when casting onto islands slopes and is hard for any feeding carp to dislodge. I'm also convinced that the loud splash attracts fish and I'll often get a bite within seconds of the feeder

Little John is home to some lovely fish!

Win On The Waggler!

01 Regular feeding with a catapult is vital!

02 Hooking fish in the top lip is a sign they're feeding right.

03 A Maver Pellet Bander makes baiting up more efficient!

04 Just a single swivel offers a slow fall and reduces twist.

settling! I use a short 9ft Maver Reactorlite rod, which is very soft, to keep hook-pulls to a minimum. Main line is 0.245mm Dual Band, with a 4in hooklength of 0.18 Genesis Extreme. I use a size 14 Maver CS20 hook with a hair-rigged band, which may seem rather big compared with many anglers' hook choices. However, when fish are sucking the pellets off the Method, I'm sure that they're not looking at the hook and, as you'll see, I promote using a large hook bait, too!

Wiggle Waggle

The most complex part of my waggler gear is the float choice. For short casts, up to 25 metres, I use an adapted straight peacock waggler. I always find the thickest possible peacock for maximum buoyancy and then cut the float down to a desired length for the distance that I'm casting. It's a trial-and-error process but by cutting numerous floats to different lengths, you'll find that you can choose just the right one for reaching the required distance. There's nothing more annoying than a waggler that's too heavy or light, meaning it either bounces back after hitting the clip or doesn't quite reach the distance! By making your own, you can get them perfect, and a thick peacock offers a nice balance between a straight waggler and pellet waggler.

For longer-range work, beyond 25 metres, I use a loaded-bodied waggler from Maver. This casts the distance accurately, makes an attractive splash as it lands, and acts as a bolt rig when a fish takes the bait. This is a big advantage because the small dips that often occur on this method can be difficult to hit at long range. Main line is 0.20mm Maver Jurassic, to a foot hooklength of 0.14mm Genesis Extreme and size 18 MT4 hook. Fish can examine the hook bait when fishing the waggler and, unlike the Method, I believe that fishing lighter produces more bites. My waggler setup is geared towards fishing up in the water and on the drop, so I opt to have all of the loading around the float. The only weight down the line is a tiny micro swivel to prevent hooklength twist. A little trick of mine is to lock the float with a row of six or eight shot, rather than the usual two or three big ones. This acts as a break as the waggler lands, preventing it from diving down and potentially spooking fish.

Aim to feed in front of the float before 'twitching' back.

Islands are the perfect target areas for rod and line.

Kicking Off

Unless the weather is red hot and I can see fish cruising around on the surface, I always start on the Method feeder. This allows me to quickly get some particles on the bottom and usually results in a run of early fish. Today, the island is lined with sedges, although there are several cutbacks with bare boards and bank showing. I like to start by casting to the edge of the sedges, where the water is a little deeper. A mistake that many people make is starting right up in the shallow water, which gives them nowhere to go once they've mugged their early fish. I can hopefully mug two lots of these early fish, firstly from the deeper water, before re-clipping tight across to snare a few more!

JPz – Jamie's secret hook bait!

Ovaltine binds pellets really well.

Tailored Feeding

My feeding regime is a crucial part of my rod-and-line approach. Many anglers simply cast out their feeder or waggler and sit there without feeding. Pinging with a catapult is a great trick and after an initial run of fish I get into the routine of feeding hard pellets very regularly. A little edge that I've gained is to feed 8mm pellets rather than the usual 4 or 6mms that many other anglers use. These make a really loud plop, without introducing too many particles, and constantly draw new fish into the peg. Feeding in this way primes the swim perfectly for the waggler and any bait that makes it to the bottom keeps fish grubbing around for the Method feeder. As the session wears on, I've normally created a fairly large area by feeding in this way, drawing a lot of fish from other anglers. Why would a carp want to feed in open water under somebody else's pole when it could feed as far away from danger as possible, against the cover of the island?

Tricks Of The Trade

As with many methods of fishing, it's the little things that make all the difference within my tactics. Hook baits are something that people generally pay little attention to on

Flicking the rod tip twitches the hook bait and triggers more bites.

the Method feeder. In the past, I've fallen into the trap of using a plain 6mm pellet in a band and thinking nothing of it when I've stopped getting bites. However, I've recently realised that hook baits can make a big difference, just as they do when fishing the pole! My starting bait on the Method is nearly always an 8mm hard pellet. I'm sure that you catch the bigger fish with a large hook bait. A favourite change bait of mine is an 8mm Marukyu JPz pellet. This is an extremely bright and smelly hook bait that stands out like a sore thumb over a bed of pellets on the Method!

I also favour a large hook bait on the waggler and believe that an 8mm pellet leads to fewer missed bites. Even when targeting carp around the 1lb mark, I've found that with an 8mm pellet you hit nearly every bite, and many of them pull the rod round! A JPz makes a great change bait on the waggler too. Slipping one on can catch you that extra fish every hour, often the difference between making the frame and falling just short!

Swapping Rods

There are no hard-and-fast rules about when to change between the Method and waggler. The key is to constantly switch between the two to keep fish coming. As a general rule, the Method is great when there are loads of fish in the peg and you can feed heavily with plenty of loose pellets. As the fish become wary, you'll find that the bigger specimens come off the bottom and, more often than not, you'll begin to catch smaller, more gullible fish. At this point, I'd think about slowing down the feed and ping in just three or four pellets every 30 seconds. Hopefully this creates competition and I'd be able to keep fish coming by switching to the waggler.

The Session

Today has been the ideal session to demonstrate my two-rod approach. I've started by casting to some sedges and after losing my first fish I've had three small mirrors in three casts! After five minutes with no indications, I've already started pinging in 8mm pellets, which has instantly brought liners and another two carp. A quiet spell urges me to try casting tight against the boards slightly to the right, where some of my loose-fed pellets have been landing. Another run of fish proves that the tactics have worked, with a welcome ghost carp of around 6lb also falling into my trap!

Things have slowed on the Method and, had this been a match, I'd expect many anglers to be reaching for their poles. Instead, I've picked up my waggler rod and eased off the amount of pellets that I'm feeding. By doing this, competition is created and a run of noticeably bigger fish than usual have hit the net. Timing is crucial on the waggler and I like to get into the routine of feeding before I cast to bring some fish into the area. If no bites come as the float sets, I'll feed again just in front of it, before twitching my hook bait by flicking the rod tip. This is a great habit to get into and will drastically increase the amount of fish that you catch on the waggler. It's a similar effect to lifting and dropping a hook bait on the pole.

When fishing against an island, I prefer to set my float at roughly the full depth. This way, I can catch any fish off the bottom as my pellet is falling through the water, but also stand a chance of catching as the

A two-rod approach is a winning tactic all year round!

Method Madness!

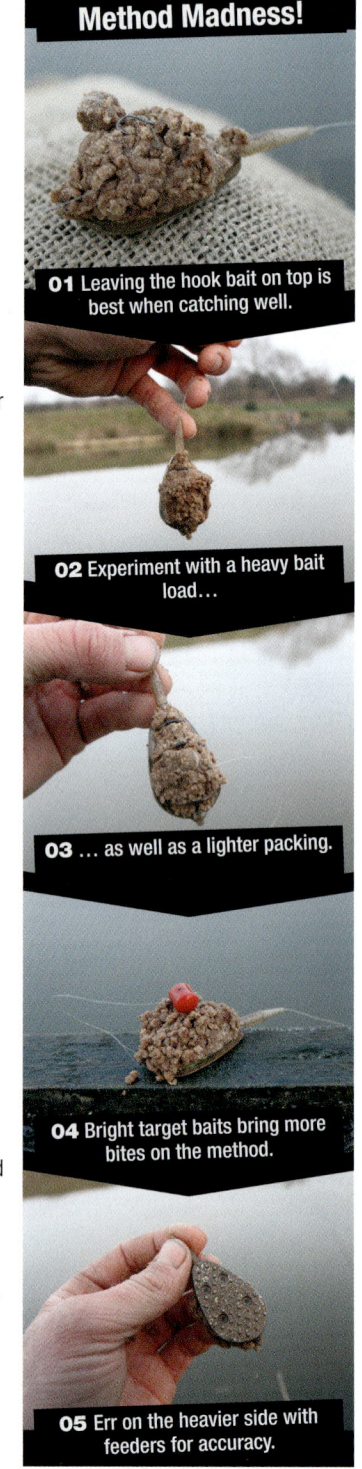

01 Leaving the hook bait on top is best when catching well.

02 Experiment with a heavy bait load…

03 … as well as a lighter packing.

04 Bright target baits bring more bites on the method.

05 Err on the heavier side with feeders for accuracy.

bait settles on the bottom. As the session's progressed, my peg's gone through spells of having lots of fish present to short, quiet periods where they seem to wise up. By strategically alternating between both rods with a tailored feeding pattern, I've managed to put together over 80lb! Ringing the changes with hook baits has resulted in several big ghosties and I've winkled out a few extra fish by casting to the left and right of my main feed area. It's a bold decision to go to a peg armed with just two rods, but by employing my advice you could be on to a winner!

Like most Pole suppliers on the map, us African grey parrots can copy most things. However, this new model is way out of any ones league!

NEW
ELITE 'ALL ROUND'

An amazing pole that boasts both quality and performance. Available at 13m & 14.5m and supplied with an excellent kit package. Maver's 'ground breaking' new slotted easy flow power kits will revolutionise the way anglers elasticate their poles.

The name itself summarises just how good this highly versatile pole actually is on canals, rivers, lakes and of course - commercials. The superior rigidity & balance allows you to fish up to 16m for much longer periods.

ELITE Made in Italy **ALL**

MAVER ELITE - ALL ROUND
The Ultimate pole

Simply breath taking innovation and technology once again from the World's biggest & best pole producer.

The NEW 'All round' is built to match the strength of the record selling 'Elite carp' but boasts the following advantages -

- Superior balance
- Unrivalled rigidity & tip speed
- Sensational handling at 14.5m - 16m
- Ultra slim/ULTRA strong sections
- Reinforced put-over female joints
- Unique teflon coated male joints (sec 3,4,5)
- Magic step technology inside power tips
- Fusion 'Easy flow' power kits.
- Sun core & Anti-friction surface throughout

NEW ALL ROUND SSP £1650.00
13m SPECIAL INTRODUCTORY OFFER
ONLY £899.99

All this state of the art technology should retail at £2200 (13m) & £2400 (14.5m)

NEW ALL ROUND SSP £1799.99
14.5m SPECIAL INTRODUCTORY OFFER
ONLY £999.99

The 'All round' Package
- 4 x Easy Flow Slotted Power Kits (inc. kit supplied in pole)
- Mini Extension
- Clean Caps • DVD
- Cupping Kit & Cups
- Quality Holdall & Protective Tubes

14.5m Extension - SSP £185.00
16.0m Extension - SSP £199.99

Maver's 'ground breaking' new slotted easy flow power kits will revolutionise the way anglers elasticate their poles. Combine with our 'easy flow' cone bungs for the ultimate elastication system.

Check out our website today for our latest news!
FIND OUT MORE
We're on facebook

FOR FULL DETAILS VISIT WWW.MAVER.CO.UK

MAVER UK 20th ANNIVERSARY

MAVER.CO.UK
THE WORLDS NUMBER 1 MATCH BRAND
UNIT 8 MERSE ROAD, NORTH MOONS MOAT IND. ESTATE, REDDITCH, WORCS B98 9HL

+44 (0) 1527 406300   info@maver.co.uk   www.maver.co.uk

UNDERSTANDING THE PELLET FEEDER

GET ON THE PELLET FEEDER

Joe Carass knows more than a thing or two about catching carp on the feeder. Here he shows you how to get the most from his favourite approach.

It is very easy to become confused as to which feeder to choose for carp fishing. There is the ever-reliable Method, the banjo and the underused pellet feeder. Each has a use and all are awesome carp catchers in their own right. However, I am going to focus on the pellet feeder.

In my opinion, it's the best of the lot! I have used it for years on the quiet and I believe that it has been one of my biggest edges. It allows you to present a small pile of pellets with your hook bait right among it – the perfect trap, you could say!

The History

Firstly, let's look at the history of this approach. It was the brainchild of none other than Andy Findlay. He came up with the simple idea when he realised that the Method feeder seemed to be losing its effectiveness on Makins. He then developed this brilliant device and the pellet feeder was born. The carp had simply not seen this type of feeder before and it went on to take the venue apart, just like the Method did on its inception.

The first pellet feeders were simply made out of old top-kit tubes and were fairly rough and ready. It wasn't until Preston Innovations took it on and designed a shop-ready version that the pellet feeder was brought into the public domain. Because I am always looking for an edge, I decided to give them a go and the rest, as they say, is history!

Why Is It So Effective?

The pellet feeder is brilliant when you want to target smaller fish. Those in the 1lb to 3lb bracket are perfectly suited to this approach. The feeder is extremely quick to load and works perfectly every single time. This makes it brilliant for speed fishing situations at smaller venues like Lindholme, where short casts are needed and plenty of fish are the target.

It is also deadly during winter. There are some very small designs available that allow you to feed much less; bait that you would use even on the smallest of Method feeders. It is far easier to regulate how much bait you are feeding with the pellet feeder.

Deep water is also an area where it excels. On some fisheries the pellets that you have to use are a little bit on the puffy side. This obviously makes them very difficult to mould around a Method feeder and they certainly won't stay on when cast into deep water. If you press them into a pellet feeder, though, you can be sure that your feeder is reaching the bottom intact.

My favourite situation for this style of feeder is when chucking

The pellet feeder makes minimal splash when cast.

Submerge your tip and pull the line to sink it.

Joe Carass
Age: 25
Lives: Daventry
Sponsor: None
Team: Ultimate Barnsley Blacks

Packington Somers
Meriden, Warwickshire
CV7 7PL
t: 01676 523833
w: www.packingtonestate.net

A small Quickchange bead allows speedy hooklength changes.

Various-sized pellet feeders allow for different feed rates.

tight to, or even into, dense far-bank vegetation. If you think about it, if you cast a Method into the undergrowth the chances are that some of the bait will get knocked off. Because the pellet feeder encapsulates your bait it gives the whole setup a degree of protection and the feeder can be cast into the vegetation with the confidence that your presentation is still perfect.

Which Feeder?

I must say that I don't just use one brand of pellet feeder. I use a mix of Preston, Guru and Garbolino feeders and also have several that I make myself. The three brands' feeders are all slightly different in size. What I am generally looking for is one that carries the same amount of bait as the pole pot that I would expect to use. So, in winter, when a small bottle top of pellets is enough, my own feeders made from a thin quivertip tube are the ones. In spring a small Preston feeder is my choice because it represents about the same as a small Cad Pot of pellets. Finally, the Guru and Garbolino models are used in summer, when I want to feed plenty of bait and really get the fish competing.

Interestingly, although I undoubtedly prefer an elasticated Method feeder to an inline model, I only use inline pellet feeders. They offer less in the way of fuss on my rig and, because they are quite light, hook-pulls are rarely an issue, as they can be on a Method feeder.

One strength of the pellet feeders is how compact they are. This means that they cast extremely well and, provided they are feathered in, enter the water very quietly. This is crucial when the water temperatures drop because carp become very sensitive to noise.

The Tackle

My setup is about as simple and hassle-free as it could possibly be. As I said, I stick to inline feeders. These are simply threaded onto a small length of twisted mono. To attach my hooklength I use a Korum Quickchange bead because this is nice and compact and allows me to change my hooklengths quickly.

The hooklength is simply a 3in (or four if rules state) length of mono. The diameter that I use might surprise people because I am a firm believer that fishing light gets you more bites, even on the feeder. For this reason, I fish 0.11mm or 0.13mm hooklengths. This goes hand in hand with my target-sized fish and I am convinced that it gets me more bites.

As far as hooks are concerned, I look to use a size 18 B911 X-Strong Eyed. This is a strong hook that is relatively lightweight, despite its strength. Other good hooks to try are the Preston PR 36 and Guru MWG, both in an 18. I have hooklengths tied up with hair-rigged bait bands but also without a hair so that I can fish maggots should I need to.

The stamp of fish again determines the rod and reel choice. My rod is a 9-10 Daiwa Match Winner, which features a pencil-thin blank and super-soft action. This goes hand in hand with chucking a small pellet feeder tight to far-bank features.

The pellet feeder is ideal for F1s.

My reel is the ever-reliable Shimano Aero Spinning 4000, which is loaded with 6lb Tournament ST main line.

Bait Choices

I have tried different sizes of pellets and even groundbait in a pellet feeder but I have come to the conclusion that 2mm pellets are the best feed. It is important how you prepare them, though, and I have a simple way of ensuring that

Loading The Feeder

01 Scoop up a small amount of pellets and press gently.

02 Tuck the line into the pellets and press.

03 Put the hook bait at the top of the opening.

04 In goes another small pinch of pellets.

05 The whole thing is then squeezed.

06 The finished feeder, done in a matter of seconds.

they are correct. It is vital that you don't overwet your pellets because they will end up becoming lodged inside the feeder. I only soak them lightly so that as soon as they enter the water they start to expand, thus spilling out from the feeder.

There is no need to add sticky pellet powders but, being a flavour freak, I will always add a small glug to my feed. Today I have opted for Mainline Cell, which has a beautiful coconut aroma. Steve Ringer put me on to this stuff and I now use it an awful lot!

There are four hook baits that I look to use and all of them depend on what I am catching. The first is the ever-dependable banded hard pellet. A 4mm or 6mm pellet is a great hook bait, especially when the venue is fishing well.

If things are a bit tricky I will swap to two hair-rigged 4mm expanders. These are a bit softer and can get a few bites on harder days.

Thirdly, dead red maggots can be a brilliant hook bait. I fish these either singly or doubly but they are fantastic, especially if the venue holds a lot of F1s and skimmers.

Finally, punched meat is a definite winner. A 6mm punch of plain meat is always good, especially if there are a few larger mirrors kicking about and you maybe need to pick the odd better fish out. Always take at least three hook baits to give you options.

Tips And Tricks

I have a few extra little gems that will catch those extra fish. The first is to plumb up your feeder swim! This is something that I learnt from fishing Molands at Packington Somers. The far bank offers little in the way of depth and I have seen so many anglers cast as tight as they can with little or no thought to what depth they are fishing in. When targeting F1s I feel that the minimum depth of water to cast in is two feet, but preferably three! They definitely prefer a bit of water over their heads. To help me settle on a depth I simply attach a small pole float onto my line and cast a lead around until I find where the depths are. This may only be a small tip but it really can make the difference.

The second tip is to watch your tip like a hawk. I have noticed that quite often you will cast in and get lots of indications for a few seconds and then they will stop. It is important not to leave the feeder too long without a proper pull because I fully believe that the fish rush in, eat all of the bait and back off. So if you are casting and getting quick indications, assume that every bit of bait is being eaten. This is normally a sign to either increase the amount of times you are casting, or even your feeder size to feed more bait.

Thirdly, the use of a pop-up hook bait. This is quite important in winter and spring because you can often be casting to dead or dying reed beds. I have experienced it so many times where I will get indications but no proper bites, only to reel in and my hook is snarled up in decaying matter! By fishing a small, popped-up dry expander pellet you can get round this because the hook bait will always hover above the pellet feeder and ensure that you are fishing correctly.

Fourthly, I always fish two or three swims. Again I plumb up the peg and find a few spots that are the same depth. This allows me to rotate swims to keep bites coming. This is particularly important in spring and summer when I treat the pellet feeder just like I would when fishing pellets on the pole. Don't be afraid to start a new line, too.

The Session

My short session today has seen me on my favourite pellet-feeder venue, Molands Mere at Packington. This is a hard water (not helped by it being frozen this morning) but the rewards are there for anglers who are prepared to work hard. This place is all about the small feeder and casting to several spots. Finding the right depth is crucial. I have managed to get bites while pleasure anglers all around the lake are blanking, proving how good this approach is.

The pellet feeder really is something that you need in your armoury and I know for sure that if you embrace it, it will put more fish in your net!

A soft-actioned rod is ideal for F1s and pellet-feeder fishing.

Despite the freezing conditions, the pellet feeder got Joe among the fish.

Molands proved a tough nut to crack, but the pellet feeder brought bites when everything else failed.

RINGER'S COMMERCIAL MASTERCLASS!

Steve Ringer
Age: 35
Lives: Northampton
Sponsors: Daiwa, Guru
Team: None

FANTASTIC FIVE!

Steve Ringer divulges five of his greatest commercial-fishery secrets gleaned from competing in major competitions.

Over the years, I've been lucky enough to compete at the highest level on commercial fisheries. Information and advice is widely available nowadays, and gaining that winning edge has become more difficult than ever. However, the extra knowledge I have gathered from fishing big-money events such as White Acres festivals, the Fish 'O' Mania final and the Parkdean Masters final has enabled me to stay one step ahead. Here are some of the tricks I have, until now, had up my sleeve…

'Pinging' pellets is a killer tactic.

Hard Stuff

On many of today's commercials, a great winning method involves fishing large, 8mm hard pellets on the bomb, loose feeding the same over the top. This is particularly effective because you avoid the attention of small fish such as silvers and F1s, and when you get a bite it's normally from a 'proper' carp. However, over the last year or so I've had a massive amount of success by replicating these bomb-and-pellet tactics on the pole.

Feeding is key with this method, and that key lies within the old adage of "little and often." Pinging just three or four 8mm pellets twice every minute is the perfect pattern. The idea is to feed twice with fewer pellets, as opposed to just once with more pellets.

I believe the carp hear the first lot of pellets hitting the water and move in. They then see the second lot falling through the water and follow them down to the hook bait. If I don't get a bite within a minute, I'll repeat the process and feed again.

It's also important to play around with presentation; try lifting and dropping the rig, and also pulling out the whole rig before laying it back in again. One will usually outfish the other on a given day. Working out these minor details puts you ahead of other anglers who simply ship out and fire pellets at their float all day!

Another vital area of focus when fishing this method is tackle. Many anglers fish lines and hooks that are too light and too small, in my opinion. I opt for an out-and-out carp rig, with 0.19mm Guru N-Gauge main line to a 6in 0.17mm hooklength of the same material. The hook is an eyed size 18 Guru MWG tied using a knotless knot, with a hair-rigged micro bait band sitting just off the back of the bend. My shotting pattern is my favourite strung bulk of No9s with the bottom shot placed eight inches from the hook and the rest spaced at 1in intervals above this. Elastic is nearly always black Hydro, perfect for landing large big carp quickly.

Aim to have the banded pellet sitting just off the bend of the hook.

TOP TIP

When fishing hard pellets on the pole I always set my rigs to fish dead depth. If a carp so much as breathes on my pellet it will then register on the float, hopefully ending up in my net!

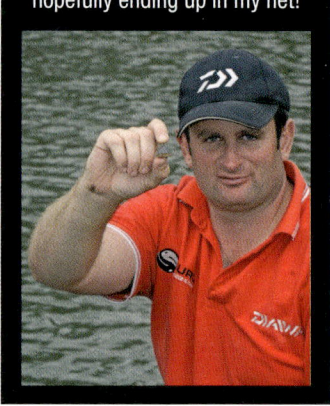

Big carp love crushing up hard pellets!

Steve is adamant that wise fish come to regular noise.

Meat Finder

You will often encounter days when carp are in the swim but aren't keen on getting their heads down. This happened to me a great deal last year, not just in the summer, but particularly in spring and autumn.

Unless carp are actively feeding on the bottom they are rarely found there, and prefer to swim up in the warmer layers of water. In such instances it would be all too easy to sit and catch just the odd fish through a session, as many anglers do!

After suffering liners and knowing the fish were present in the swim on several outings, I decided to try a shallow approach… but with a difference. It's what I call fishing 'deep shallow' and has caught me a lot of fish over the years, particularly in the cool weather. It involves fishing anywhere from three feet deep to just a foot off the bottom.

Float choice is a Mick Wilkinson Diamond, the size matched to the depth I'm fishing. As a starting point, if fishing six feet deep I'd opt for a 0.4g float. Main line is 0.19mm Guru N-Gauge to a 6in hooklength of 0.17mm in the same material. Hook bait is normally a hair-rigged 6mm cube on a size 18 Guru MWG. My shotting pattern is a strung bulk of No8s, the bottom one 18 inches from the hook, and the rest spaced at 1in intervals above.

A catapult is the best way of feeding with this method, but instead of the pinged pellets I mentioned before I much prefer meat. This is a highly visible and incredibly slow-falling bait. Pinging in just three cubes over the float every 30 seconds or so is the way to go. This isn't a lot, but just enough to create a column of slow-falling bait and oils to attract the midwater carp.

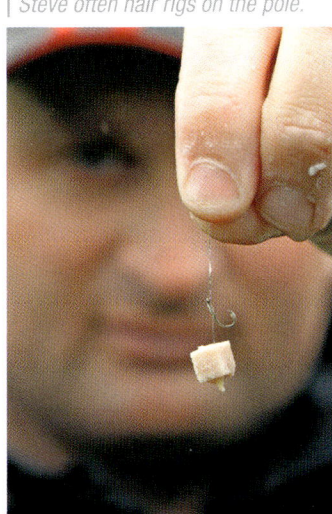

By only feeding three cubes at a time, if I want to go back on the deck later on I will still be able to because I won't have overfed the swim. The key is to stick at the method, and regularly change depths by a foot. You'll often find that fish come in runs of three or four, as they're drawn into the column. With a strict feeding regime, and regular depth changes, fishing deep shallow is certainly something that can turn an average peg into a flyer!

| The biggest carp cruise well off the bottom.

Meat… oily, highly visible and extremely slow sinking.

| Steve often hair rigs on the pole.

Liking It Late!

Commercial carp are becoming increasingly clued up to anglers' tactics. They're now wise to times of the day and certain feeding strategies, and you have to really think outside the box to trick them. Big-potting groundbait down the edge has been a great example of this.

I was never really able to get this tactic to work, which I found frustrating to say the least! Looking back, I think there are two reasons why I struggled. Firstly, I feel that I fed the wrong mix. I thought that you could pretty much pot in any groundbait and the carp would come over it. Although they did do this, actually catching them proved impossible until I switched to feeding a much coarser mix in the form of Dynamite Baits Sweet Fishmeal. I believe this mix was so successful because of the bigger particles that it contains. They had the effect of keeping the carp feeding for longer, increasing the chances of my hook bait being picked up.

I also found that adding particles such as dead maggots to the mix and then fishing a bunch of dead reds on the hook made a big difference. This got the carp used to feeding on the maggots, so my hook bait didn't stand out quite so much.

Another key thing I learnt was that potting in a couple of balls wasn't enough. The key is to put a lot of bait in all in one go, and mimic someone packing away. Timing here is crucial, and I'll often not even consider doing it until two hours before the end of the match. Up to 15 big pots of groundbait seems a much better approach than feeding at regular intervals with small amounts. Other anglers feeding groundbait early might catch the odd daft fish before you, but by waiting you'll have a burst of the bigger, wiser fish in the last hour!

Keepnet Line

Another little trick that I picked up last year is to fish what I call the 'keepnet line'. I fished a match at Makins and drew next to an angler who I couldn't seem to shake off – we were pretty much fish for fish throughout the match. Athough I felt I just had the edge weightwise, with 15 minutes to go both of us ground to a halt.

He then picked up a different rig and replumbed on a top kit straight in front of him, basically between his nets! The next thing I noticed was that he threw four massive handfuls of bait in on this line and went straight over the top with his rig. My initial thought was that it wouldn't work – only to look back 30 seconds later to see his elastic out! I thought it was a one-off fluke, only for him to land three carp for the best part of 20lb, pipping me by 7lb!

Since that day I have adopted the tactic and it has more than proved its effectiveness. I think the reason it works so well is that throwing in a large quantity of bait so late on again gives the carp the impression that it's an angler packing up.

You might now be thinking: "Why not just do it down the edge?" Well, for me, the reason it's so effective is that it's in the slightly deeper water straight in front of the platform, an area where carp are used to finding bait.

F1 Tuning

F1s can be one of the trickiest species to master. A lot of venues are absolutely solid with them nowadays and knowing how to catch them is essential to winning! Just about every venue that has F1s in has been densely stocked. For that reason they are always in your peg, wherever you draw. The nature and size of these fish means that venue owners stock a lot more of them than other types of carp. When I hear of anglers moaning about not drawing very well I immediately think that the fish were probably in their pegs anyway!

I've had days where the depth that I think is correct to fish leads to no bites at all, and you could be forgiven for thinking that there are no fish in your peg. A simple adjustment to the depth, however, can see you catch a fish every cast! Snake lakes allow you to go further up the island shelf until you have located the fish, meaning you can explore different

| *Three of these in the final 20 minutes can make a big difference!*

| *Steve has learnt to wait and target the margins late in a match.*

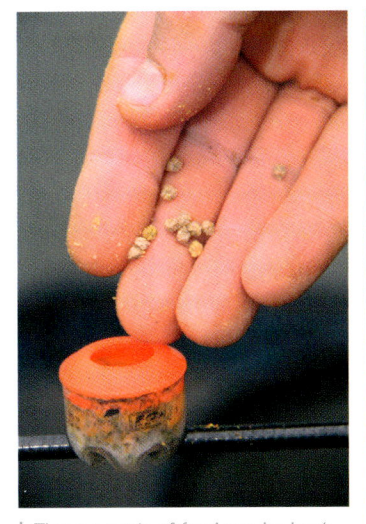

Tiny amounts of feed can be best.

Three simple baits suffice for F1s!

Gain an edge by dyeing your pellets.

Mick Wilkinson Slims – Steve's number-one choice for F1s.

bang down the middle and on others they are right across the lake in the shallow water. By just making a mental note of this before the start I give myself a little bit of a head start by going to where I think the fish are.

Maggots, pellets and corn are my three favourite baits for F1s. However, the ways in which I feed each of these are very different. With maggots appealing to every species you need to feed slightly more than other baits, as silver fish will no doubt eat a certain amount of the maggots that you have fed. For my standard lines, where I am fishing in the shallower water, I look to feed 10 to 15 maggots every cast via a small pot on my pole. This is just enough to allow me to gauge the response and I can increase or decrease the amount depending on how many fish I am catching or indications I am getting.

Be careful when you increase the feed, though, as often it draws in

depths while still fishing on the deck. Make sure you use any shelves or slopes to your advantage!

When I first get to my peg I also apply watercraft to help me decide where to start my match. F1s have a habit of topping a lot before the match starts. Usually a pattern develops as to where they are topping; some days they will be

a lot of small silvers that can be a nuisance, so it is always best to feed as little as possible.

Pellets are the best bait for chasing the fish around your peg, as they are so instant. By this I mean if it is a day where the fish are constantly on the move then I know that I can plumb up a new line, tap in six pellets and get an instant response. A quick way to get off to a good start is to fish a line short at, say, five metres, and feed just a few pellets. You will normally get a good start here before bites tail off. When this does happen you need to quickly move and start again as the F1s won't come back to a pellet line like they will a maggot line. A small pot with a pepper-pot-type lid is

great for this as it allows you to fill it up and feed three or four pellets, sit and wait for a bite and then repeat. It saves you shipping back between feeds, as pellets falling through the water column will spark a response. I also like to dye my pellets yellow, to give me something different, potentially an edge over the opposition!

When fishing corn, I like to feed just three grains and a tiny pinch of pellets. With corn being fairly small-fish proof I know that it is getting to the bottom where I can sit and wait. The good thing with corn is that you get a quick, positive bite and a neatly hooked fish.

F1s play an important role in matches.

TAP THE BALL OF PELLETS IN... THE BAIT GOES STRAIGHT TO THE BOTTOM...

Callum Dicks
Age: 23
Lives: Bristol
Sponsor: Maver
Team: Daiwa Dorking

KEEP THEM DOWN

We task **Callum Dicks** to show you how to get the most from a far-bank snake-lake swim when liners become a nightmare.

The far side of any commercial snake lake is arguably the most prolific area of your swim. With angling pressure the fish naturally push to the far side of the lake and it is there that you must target if you want consistent results!

The ideal scenario to look for in a typical summer match would be a bare bank where as little as six inches of water can be found. This 'mud' line can be extremely productive and the fish you catch over there are quite often a much bigger stamp. However, not every peg is a 'dream' draw and quite often you are faced with a far-bank swim that is less than perfect for what you are trying to do.

Here at Acorn Lakes you always have a bare bank to fish against. This is usually a gap in the sedges and normally a couple of feet wide. However, the far ledge on this lake means that finding a flat or gently sloping bottom is nearly impossible. Instead you are faced with two feet of water tight against the far bank, which is not ideal.

This is a situation that we are seeing more often these days. As commercials become older the banks are becoming more and more undercut. This means that whereas once before we had lovely

Acorn Fishery
Kingston Seymour,
Near Bristol
t: 01934 834050
w: www.acornfishery.com

Callum's approach makes these easy to catch.

Small skimmers were the first fish to show.

shallow ledges to fish on, deep hollows now replace them!

There are several ways to get round this, though, and hopefully today you will see that you can still catch a decent net of carp even when faced with plenty of depth. First up is perhaps the most conventional approach, but I put my own twist on things.

A pretty standard method here is to feed 2mm pellets through a pole pot and use a 4mm expander on the hook. This is a great way of getting bites and it does win plenty of matches, particularly in spring. But as soon as the water warms up, fishing in this manner can be a nightmare. The fish are all too willing to come off the bottom and in such shallow water catching up in the water is difficult. The only option is to try and force the fish to the bottom.

Firstly I'll talk about bait. As I said, 2mm pellets are deadly but I go about things a bit differently, though. I use the Nash 2mm Sticky Method Pellets and combine them with a hand full of even smaller 1mm versions. This pellet mix is then dampened and soaked for about two minutes before I drain all of the water from them. This leaves you with perfect pellets that can be made into hard balls.

These hard balls are what I feed to get the fish to go straight to the bottom. In my experience loose pellets only send the fish wild and make liners a nightmare. My sticky alternatives are totally different, though. I make small balls about the size of a 50p coin and feed one of these every time I ship across. I then accurately position my hook bait over the top and wait. Granted you won't get

An awesome net of fish!

Fish as tight to the far bank as possible.

anywhere near the amount of indications with this approach, but what you will get is cleaner, more positive bites that lead to properly hooked fish.

The only problem I had when first adopting this approach was how to draw the fish into the peg. I am fully aware that falling bait draws the fish in and with my balls of pellets going straight to the bottom, falling bait isn't a factor. To get round this I rely on noise. I always 'plop' my pellets in from a height of about two feet. This seems to 'ring the dinner bell' and quite often a quick bite will be the result.

The rigs that I use for this kind of approach really are simple; I find it more important to get your feeding right than having any kind of fancy rig!

I fish with two of the very best anglers, in Will Raison and Des Shipp, and both of them have taught me that having reliable end tackle is a must. For this reason I use sturdy and robust 0.18mm Genesis main line to a 6in trace of 0.14mm. This is relatively heavy for the size of fish I'm going to be catching but I know that nothing is going to let me down.

The same goes for my hook choice; a size 16 Maver CS21 is a strong pattern that suits my 4mm or 6mm expander perfectly. My float is a 0.2g Elite series 9 pattern, a lovely, short, no-frills float and ideal for the job in hand. My elastic choice may surprise people in that it is a rather light 6-10 Dual Core Retro. This elastic stretches for miles, but combine that with the strong line and strong hook and it becomes very difficult to lose fish! It also allows smaller fish to be landed, which all helps in the weight-building process.

Today has been a great example of my simple yet deadly approach. My peg offered the usual two feet of water tight across and with it being so warm I knew the fish would be looking to come up in the water at any sign of loose bait!

I simply fed and fished straightaway with the Kinder pot. There was no need to big pot bait over there as the fish were already in the peg.

After a slow initial 10 minutes with just a handful of small skimmers to show for my efforts, slowly the feeding pattern came good and I was into a steady run of carp. Here at Acorn 80lb to 120lb is likely to be needed for a win, which means catching over 50 fish. This is only 10 an hour and when they are coming as fast as they are today you can see why it is easy to build a weight.

It is also easy to get it wrong, though, and a spell of foul-hookers can quite easily ruin your rhythm. Just keep going and feeding and the runs of proper bites will come.

I call time on my short session and after three hours I have well over the 100lb mark! Hopefully you can see my approach is very simple but it is devastating and, better still, anyone can do it!

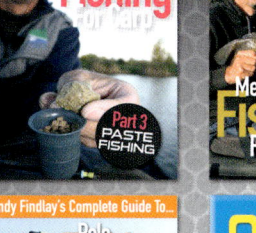

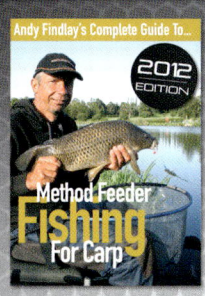

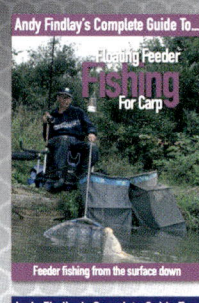

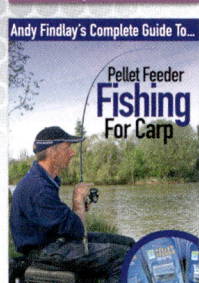

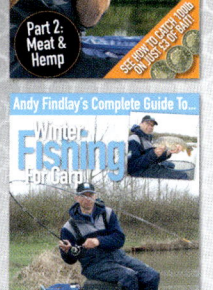

CATCH MORE CARP ON BREAD!

Cross Drove Fishery
Hockwold, Norfolk
t: 01842 828102

Mark Pollard
Age: 48
Lives: Bedford
Sponsors: Shimano, Dynamite Baits
Team: Stanjay Tackle

THE ART OF DOBBING

Mark Pollard is a master of the art of 'dobbing', so we caught up with him to see just how he goes about catching a netful on just a few slices of bread.

Dobbing is very much the 'in' approach these days. Every commercial venue you visit seems to have anglers feeding no bait yet reaping the rewards with plenty of fish.

It is a simple approach based around watercraft, location and presentation. Get it right and you could have the best winter's day ever; get it wrong, though, and you could leave the bank feeling a little bit frustrated!

Since becoming a full-time angler I had to quickly adapt my fishing to keep the match wins coming. One of the methods that I had to get to grips with was dobbing. Coming from a background of canal and river fishing, the fact that I could catch a load of fish without feeding seemed horrendously alien to me – I'm used to feeding a swim carefully all day to catch.

However, I knew that if I was to keep up my consistency I would have to get dobbing sorted. First of all I decided to ask a few anglers who already knew a bit about this approach. They all had different theories on depths and baits but it gave me a starting point. I have since gone on to win loads of matches on this super simple method and I thought I would share my findings with you.

Location Is Paramount

This was the biggest thing that I learnt along the way. In winter, carp will rarely move onto loose feed. As much as I have tried I have come to realise that YOU have to find the fish, not the other way around, as it can be in summer. This means searching every inch of your swim.

Today I am at Cross Drove Fishery on a typical peg. It has an island in front of me plus a channel to my left with dense marginal reeds. There is also lots of open water to search. Usually in winter I will look to target features when dobbing. The island in front of me and the channel to my left both give me plenty of options in terms of hiding holes for the carp.

However, on some days the fish will much prefer to be in the open water and I cannot rule out the need to look here at some point.

My starting line will generally be where I think will be the best spot, and today that is to the island in front of me. Prior knowledge of this peg has helped me in this respect. Because you are not feeding anything, though, it is easy to just try somewhere new and that is the beauty of this approach. You will catch whatever is present and not spoil your peg with feed.

Depth Is Key

Almost as important as location is the depth that you fish at. I fully believe that carp sit off the bottom in winter so it makes sense to present your hook bait right in front of their mouths. Many of the anglers that I spoke to suggested fishing at half depth. This was what I tried but it just didn't seem right to me and I didn't catch. The best depth I have found is between three and six inches off the bottom. This gives you the best chance of catching fish at all layers – if the fish do happen to be sat off the bottom then I will catch them on the drop, but if they

F1s are suckers for bread!

Polly stores his spare slices in a bag.

Search all of your swim – the carp will be hiding somewhere!

Expect some big fish so gear up accordingly.

Two slices of bread – 60lb of carp!

are close to the bottom the hook bait still reaches them.

By all means try fishing shallower, and it makes sense to work to your indications. If on some days you are getting a lot of indications but few bites then try shallowing up. This can sometimes be the case when you are sitting on a shedload of carp!

The Right Bait

For me the only bait to use when dobbing is bread. I can see the merit of using corn or maggots but I have found that bread is number one and will always get me a few bites. I think it is the visual factor that appeals to me the most, a swollen piece of bread is a highly visible offering that is also super-soft and easy for an inquisitive carp to eat.

Typically I will use a large punch of about 8mm as I have found this deters the unwanted attentions of roach but isn't too big so that smaller carp will ignore it. There are so many F1s about these days that you also have to bear these in mind, so the 8mm seems about the right size as a compromise hook bait.

To prepare the bait I simply give it a 10-second blast in the microwave and then store the slices in a plastic bag. This gives the slices a slight tackiness but doesn't make them too firm. In my experience the bread doesn't want any firm bits in it whatsoever. The hook seems to struggle to strike through these and more often than not the bite can be missed.

One little trick I do to keep the slice from drying out is to place it in a bait tub and then place another bait tub on top of it when I have punched out my hook bait. This prevents the air getting to it and keeps the slice perfect.

Reliable Rigs

Despite my canal background and use of delicate lines and small hooks, you would be surprised to learn that I think it is much better to use strong gear. The lightest line I would ever consider using when dobbing is 0.14mm and would be much happier using 0.16mm or even 0.18mm! When you're fishing with bread the fish rarely seem tackle-shy and you often catch some huge carp, so I see no point in risking getting broken.

The same goes for hooks, where a size 16 B911 X-Strong Spade is my number-one choice. They are super-sharp and super-strong, which allows me to land everything that I hook.

My favourite floats are old MP4 floats in a 3x8 size and I shot them with a simple bulk of Stotz 10 inches from the hook. It is important to have a float with a bristle capable of supporting your hook bait. By this I mean choose a hollow bristle with a decent thickness that is not only buoyant but also visible when tucking it into various spots.

The old-faithful white Hydro finishes the setup nicely. This elastic allows me to land even the biggest carp, as it possesses plenty of stretch.

The Result

As you can see, my setup and approach are unbelievably simple. It is so important to get the simple things right and I urge you to try it. Dobbing really is simple but the rewards are massive if you get things right!

FLOAT SPECIALISTS

MALKO FLOATS
- ALL HANDCRAFTED USING THE BEST BALSA MATERIALS
- COMPACT BODY
- GREAT STABILITY /STRENGTH

NEW RANGE OF FLOATS

RRP £1.50 EACH

TAILORMADE FLOATS TO SUIT YOU
CALL US ON: 07971 799453
FOLLOW US ON FACEBOOK

DJK Floats & Tackle
UK MADE FLOATS
djkfloats@gmail.com | Tel: 01226 744343
www.floatsandtackle.co.uk

MW FLOATS
The Originals and the Best - Only For The HardCore!

Pro Power Margin   Pro Power Paste

DESIGNED TO PERFORM
- All bodies turned inhouse by Mick Wilkinson himself
- Manufacturer of original handmade commercial-fishery pole floats

www.floatman.co.uk

malman floats
Handmade pole floats turned and finished in the UK
Only Available direct from:
www.malmanfloats.com
Email: gaz@malmanfloats.com

NG Floats
10% DISCOUNT CODE FOR READERS ON ALL PRODUCTS EXCLUDING HANDMADE FLOATS
CODE: MF10

- HANDMADE AND XT RANGE POLE FLOATS
- PELLET WAGS
- WAGGLERS
- SILICONE AND LINE

Commercial XT Range A range made to Nick Gilbert's exact specification by a top European Float Company. Available in 9 patterns, you will find a float design to cover all commercial fishing. Prices from £1.50

NG Handmade Floats Handmade by Nick Gilbert, made using high-density foam bodies that will never take on water, each float is handpainted with five coats, two of which are a 'Hard Coat' paint, unique to NG Floats. Prices from £2.00

www.float-store.co.uk / Tel: 07743 416559

Handmade floats may take up to 3 weeks delivery during busy times, XT range sent out same or next day / Card payment taken on the phone / Postage cost for orders under £15 - £1.50, orders over £15 - £2.50, orders over £100 FREE.

MB FLOATS
MB (HANDMADE) CANAL SPECIALS
HAND-FINISHED HT FOAM COMMERCIAL PATTERNS

20 YEARS HANDMADE SPECIALS

Handmade Specials since 1993
www.mbfloats.co.uk
Tel: 01455 284493 Email: mick@mbfloats.co.uk

CATCH MORE ON SLOPING VENUES

Bannister House Farm Fishery
Mere Brow, near Preston, Lancashire PR4 6JR

Jamie Hughes
Age: 29
Lives: The Wirral
Sponsors: Maver, Bag 'em
Team: Maver Midlands

SLOPING SOLUTIONS

Follow **Jamie Hughes'** expert advice to relieve the headache caused by steep-sloping swims.

As we all know, most commercial waters these days feature sloping near and far margins. Some of these are nice gradual affairs but more often than not you will be faced with a steep slope that is a nightmare to fish on. This steep slope can actually be used to your advantage and should not be something to be scared of.

One of the most frequent topics I get asked about as an angling coach is how to plumb up correctly when fishing to island features or the far side of snake lakes, and more specifically which areas to target. Most anglers will try to find the top and base of the shelf in the hope of finding the flattest spots.

While I agree that these are the correct steps and they are areas that produce well when the fish are

| *The slopes at Bannister House can cause anglers a lot of problems.*

Use positive bristles when fishing on slopes.

Use a heavy plummet for accuracy.

Use both a pot and a catty for feeding.

feeding, many anglers are missing out on fish by neglecting the water in between these two extremes. The reason they dismiss it is because it is deemed unfishable due to the gradient of the slope.

I am at a typical steep-sloping venue, Bannister House Fishery in Lancashire, to hopefully show you how to catch plenty of fish off these tricky gradients.

Accuracy Is Key

Plumbing up a sloping swim needs to be done in a very precise and accurate manner. To ensure that you are fishing in exactly the right spot, you must choose a static far-bank marker to line up against. Marking your pole section with tape or Tipp-Ex, or simply using the graphics on your pole as a reference point, will also ensure that you are fishing at the exact same distance each time.

If the wind permits, a short line of around 10 inches between float and pole tip will also help you to keep the rig in the correct place.

I use a heavy 30g plummet for a positive reading and I like to plumb up so that just the bristle of my float is visible when held on a tight line. I then plumb up six inches shorter and six inches past my chosen area, which will show me just how steep the slope is.

A good tip is to target the area directly in front of you, rather than at an angle to one side. Fishing square to the slope like this should increase your accuracy even further. The size of this zone is reduced when you fish at an angle and it also affects your feeding.

Choose The Right Float

Floats for fishing the slope are entirely up to the individual but my preferred pattern is a nice rugby-ball shape with a visible hollow bristle and wire stem, such as the Maver Elite Series 7 that I'm using. Sizes will depend entirely on the depth of the peg and conditions on the day

The shallow water on top of the shelf was very productive.

Try softening your 4mm pellets.

Accurately mark your pole once the correct spots are found.

but, generally speaking, I will use a 4x12 in depths from 18 inches to three feet, a 4x14 from three to five feet and a 4x16 for five to seven feet.

Shotting is a critical part of slope fishing and I find a tapered bulk is by far the best. It allows my hook bait to get down fairly quickly while also allowing me to use fairly large, positive shot close to the hook, such as No9s and No10s. Larger shot register better on the float when dislodged by a fish taking the bait, resulting in more positive bites.

To increase this sensitivity even further I always incorporate the weight of the hook bait into the float's shotting. In my opinion, this is the ultimate setup for bite registration because the hook bait acts as the last dropper shot – so as soon as the bait is taken it is registered on the float.

Utilising the weight of the hook bait has the added benefit of indicating if you are fishing in the correct place; position your rig too far up the slope and the float will not settle properly; too short of the slope and it will be overshotted and sink.

Perfect Pellets

I like to keep things simple, so for 99 per cent of my fishing I use pellets for feed. This suits most of my chosen venues with stockings of F1s, small carp and skimmers. Pellets are a bait that I have complete confidence in; they are fairly dense and heavy, which, in my opinion, is crucial when fishing on a sloping bottom.

For feeding in warm weather I have two options: softened 4mm feed pellets, which are ideal when skimmers and F1s are the main target, or hard 6mm pellets, which come into their own for carp from 1lb to 4lb.

Hook baits are either hard 6mm pellets or a 6mm Bag 'em expander that has been pumped in gelatine. This helps to keep the pellet on the hook but, more importantly, adds a lot of weight to the pellet, allowing it to register on the float bristle much more clearly.

Correct Feeding

Working out the best way to feed when fishing on a slope is something that I've spent a lot of time experimenting with. Understanding how easily feeding fish can disperse loose feed was the first step. Any amount of feed will usually be spread very quickly and the majority of it will be wafted down to the base of the slope.

Secondly, I took into account the ways in which the fish prefer to feed. The first and last hours of a session were producing plenty of fish in the shallowest water at the top of the slope.

During the middle three hours, however, I was putting very few fish into the net. I put this down to them being easy to catch at first when your feed is still in a tight area.

Once a few fish have been caught, though, the bait will begin to spread all over the shelf, taking the fish with it. This meant that I would struggle to catch until the last hour, when the fish would typically feed more confidently and move back up the shelf in the shallower water to compete for the feed.

Fishing lines down the slope was the obvious answer but they had to be fed carefully. I've now settled on a quick, simple way of feeding. When fishing the shallowest point of the slope I use a small pole-mounted pot to drip bait in accurately. All other depths on the slope are fed by pinging just a few pellets with a catapult.

By starting the session in the shallow water and then rotating between the middle and base of the slope later on, a much steadier catch rate is achieved… until they 'rock up' again at the top of the shelf for you to plunder in the last hour!

To book Jamie for a coaching session visit
www.fishingtuitionandcoaching.co.uk

Get to know the slopes and reap the rewards!

CATCH CARP WITH A SINKING FLOAT!

Meadowlands Fishery
Ryton-upon-Dunsmore,
Coventry, Warwickshire
CV8 3EG
t: 0121 603 0127

Darren Cox
Age: 46
Lives: Stratford-Upon-Avon
Sponsors: Garbolino
Team: Kamasan Starlets

THE SINKING WAGGLER

The sinking waggler has been one of the biggest secrets of recent years, but Darren Cox lifts the lid on this awesome tactic!

Yes, you read it correctly… the sinking waggler. It is a deadly approach that has caught me an absolute heap of carp. This approach may sound a little unorthodox but when faced with large lakes, deep water and plenty of carp then it is a definite winner.

Firstly, let's have a look at why this method is so effective. As we all know, the pellet waggler is one of the best summer approaches there is. When the method is right it can be like shelling peas; however, several years after its inception the pellet waggler seems to be losing its effectiveness, particularly in deep water where it can be a difficult method to master. When faced with so much water, finding the correct depth to fish at can be a minefield.

The sinking waggler gets round this, however, as it allows you to search the depths. When I say sinking waggler, though, it is important to say how slowly the float sinks. The float is fine-tuned so that it only just sinks when the weight of the hook bait is added. The float will then slowly 'parachute' through the swim. Because the float only just sinks, the line between the hook bait and float is completely straight. This means that the fall of the bait is incredibly slow as it is 'held up' by the float.

It is then a case of counting down your float and using the bite time

Keep your feed light but frequent.

a judge as to what depth the fish are at. The rig is a kind of warning system and swim searcher. It is ideal as you can fish at every depth of your swim with one rig!

Setting up the rig is quite simple but you do need some important items of tackle to achieve the slow sinking and fine-tuning of the float. The number-one choices for me are Garbolino Flighted Pellet Wagglers. These feature an adjustable loading at the base, which consists of several small brass discs. They come supplied perfectly weighted but by adding one or two extra discs the float will hang in the surface tension. By adding the weight of the pellet the float will just sink. It is incredibly slow and the descent to the lake bed will take 15 to 20 seconds, but that is exactly what you are looking for.

The float is fixed in place using a fixed waggler adaptor and I tend to set it three to four feet from the hook. Don't forget there will still be occasions when you will get bites before the float has had a chance to sink.

The rest of my terminal tackle is pretty standard fare, I use 3lb Maxima main line and combine this with 0.18mm Garbo Line. My hook choice is the ever-reliable Drennan Barbless Carp Feeder in a size 16. Interestingly, I only ever use a lasso when hair rigging pellets. It is a confidence thing and I just think the bait is much more secure than when using a band.

My rods are G-Max 11ft 6in commercial wagglers. These have been designed with pellet-waggler fishing in mind and the slight extra length over a normal 11ft rod gives you a bit more control. My reels are rear-drag Shimano Stradics, which I think are fantastic for waggler fishing.

Even though the sinking waggler is the boss method it is well worth

| *By searching his swim, Darren located the fish eight feet below the surface.*

having a standard pellet waggler set up. If it becomes apparent that a certain depth is where the fish are sitting then set your standard rig to that depth and fish the normal waggler. It is slightly more efficient and can speed your catch rate up, having done the hard work searching your swim with the sinker.

Finally, a bomb rod should also be at the ready. There are days where the fish simply don't want to feed shallow and in this situation the bomb is deadly. Fish it with big hook baits such as double 8mm or even double 11mm pellets and be patient.

Moving on, the next important thing to look at is bait. For feeding I tend to stick to simple 8mm coarse pellets. They are what everyone uses these days and the fish love to crunch on them! However, there are occasions when the wind can be a problem and you simply cannot fire the bait far enough. In this situation then I will look to use 11mm coarse pellets. As an absolute last resort, and providing they are allowed, I will use halibut pellets. These are denser than coarse pellets so can be fired further. The only drawback with them, though, is that they sink much faster.

When it comes to feeding I look to get into a regimented routine. The

Darren uses these brass discs to fine-tune his float.

key is to keep the pellets plopping in for the full five hours. This approach does need to be stuck to and given your full attention. Let's be honest, it is rare on big-fish venues to get more than 15 bites so you need to stick at it. You may only need three bites an hour and it takes patience and confidence. To feed the swim correctly I feed between four and eight pellets every 45 to 60 seconds ALL match. This ensures that the plopping noise is a constant as it is this that draws the fish in to the peg in the first place.

One trick that I have used a lot in the past is to quickly up the feed for 10 minutes. By this I mean start feeding very positively for a short period of time. This 'barrage' quite often sees you get a couple of quick fish.

Another thing you should always carry is a variety of hook baits. I have a small tub that has several colours and sizes of pellets to try. Sometimes a white or a very dark pellet can be excellent and can score you bites when all else fails.

Finally, a dodge that I have used to great effect is to troll the hook bait. Trolling is simple to do and is a way of slowly moving the hook bait through the swim. I simply cast out slightly further and then slowly reel the rig back towards me once the float has settled and began its descent to the bottom. And I mean slowly – the reel handle should take roughly eight to nine seconds to complete a full revolution. This not only attracts bites but it is a way of keeping a tight line between rod tip and float. This helps with hitting bites, as nine times out of 10 the rod will just arch round with a fish on.

It has been a great day today and the sinking waggler has been awesome, outfishing the standard setup quite considerably. The session has been quite tricky in that I have had to work very hard for each fish, but that is where the sinking float comes into its own and can make all the difference.

A beautiful carp caught on a great method!

GET LOADS MORE CARBON FOR YOUR MONEY!

G-MAX M1 16M POLE PACK
2 x 4.4m Match Lite Kits, 2 x 2.9m Match Lite Kits, 1 x 2.9m Power Lite Kit,
1 x 2.9m Power Puller Slot Kit, 1 x Extendable Potting Kit + Pots,
2 x Short No4 Sections, 1 x Garbolino Pole Holdall

SSP £2,499.99 — PLUS GET 3 EXTRA 2.9M POWER PULLER SLOT KITS, SAVING AN INCREDIBLE £269.97!

NOW WITH 10 TOP KITS

G-MAX M3 16M POLE PACK
1 x 4.4m Match Lite Kit, 2 x 2.9m Match Lite Kits, 2 x 2.9m Power Lite Kits,
1 x 2.9m Power Puller Slot Kit 1 x Extendable Potting Kit + Pots,
1 x Short No4 Sections, 1 x Garbolino Pole Holdall

SSP £1,829.99 — PLUS GET 3 EXTRA 2.9M POWER PULLER SLOT KITS, SAVING AN INCREDIBLE £269.97!

NOW WITH 10 TOP KITS

G-MAX M5 16M POLE PACK
1 x 4.4m Match Lite Kit, 3 x 2.9m Power Lite Kits, 1 x 2.9m Power Puller Slot Kit
1 x Extendable Potting Kit + Pots, 1 x Garbolino Pole Holdall

SSP £1,259.99 — PLUS GET 2 EXTRA 2.9M POWER PULLER SLOT KITS, SAVING AN INCREDIBLE £179.99!

NOW WITH 8 TOP KITS

G-MAX C1 14.5M POLE PACK
3 x 2.9m Power Lite Kits, 1 x 2.9m Power Puller Slot Kit, 1 x Extendable Potting Kit + Pots,
2 x Short No4 Sections, 1 x Garbolino Pole Holdall

SSP £949.99 — PLUS GET 2 EXTRA 2.9M POWER PULLER SLOT KITS, SAVING AN INCREDIBLE £179.99!

NOW WITH 7 TOP KITS

G-MAX 600 14.5M POLE PACK
3 x 2.9m Power Lite Kits, 1 x Extendable Potting Kit + Pots, 1 x Garbolino Pole Holdall

SSP £789.99 — PLUS GET 1 EXTRA 2.9M POWER PULLER SLOT KIT, SAVING AN INCREDIBLE £59.99!

NOW WITH 5 TOP KITS

G-MAX CARP 550 13M POLE PACK
3 x 2.9m Power Lite Kits, 1 x Extendable Potting Kit + Pots, 1 x Garbolino Pole Holdall

SSP £629.99 — PLUS GET 1 EXTRA 2.9M POWER PULLER SLOT KIT, SAVING AN INCREDIBLE £59.99!

NOW WITH 5 TOP KITS

SUMMER MADNESS TOP-KIT DEALS

AVAILABLE FROM ALL GARBOLINO STOCKISTS
VISIT: GARBOLINOUK.COM
For full G-MAX specifications, all Garbolino products, news and features.

WINNERS CHOOSE
garbolino — REACHING BEYOND EXPECTATIONS

WIN WITH BIG FISH

Gold Valley Lakes
Aldershot, Hampshire, GU11 2PT

t: 01252 336333
w: www.goldvalleylakes.com

Will Raison
Age: 38
Lives: Aldershot
Sponsors: Daiwa, Old Ghost
Team: Daiwa Dorking

METHOD AND MARGINS

Will Raison reveals his two-pronged attack for commercial lumps!

Nowadays, fisheries up and down the country contain lots of very big carp. After years of anglers trying to catch them, these fish have wised up to almost every trick in the book. Today I've brought you to Gold Valley Lakes in Aldershot, a venue I've been lucky enough to grow up on. The carp on this venue have grown massively. Winning weights here are always well in excess of 100lb, and this can be made up of just a dozen fish. After several warm days, dark shapes cruise around covering the surface. Many anglers come off the bank on such days having seen hundreds of pounds of fish swim past but not being able to catch them. A very positive approach involving one rod and one pole rig can be deadly when it's like this. I may only get 15 bites all day but will more often than not come away with a brown envelope. Let me tell you more…

Simplicity

Spending maximum time in the water is one of my main aims when targeting big fish. Complicating things with lots of rigs and different swims only reduces fishing time. Today I can already see a dozen or so double-figure carp lazily mooching around on the surface in front of me. Although these fish will occasionally take bait that's dangled in front of their noses, targeting them wastes a lot of time. Instead, I find it best to target the fish that actually want to feed.

Setting Traps

In the early stages of a match, finding the feeding fish can be very difficult, with only the odd fish coming into a swim to feed. To maximise my chances of hooking these fish, I focus on fishing a Method feeder. This allows me to place my hook bait right among a small ball of feed, and when a big fish does pick this up, it will more often than not hook itself. Here on Middle Lake, I've got a rope to cast at around 30 metres. I'm going to base the first part of the session

| *Will has lots of confidence adding Maggot Meal to his margin groundbait.*

| *A white hook bait stands out well and is effective on the Method.*

A bunch of maggots is deadly…

… but double corn works well too.

fishing to this feature where fish will naturally patrol. If I was faced with open water, I'd simply pick an area I could comfortably cast to, and clip up there.

Any fish with a feeding instinct will be drawn in to the noise of the feeder going in. However, rather than constantly casting, it can pay to sit and wait without creating lots of small piles of bait. Instead, simply ping the occasional 8mm pellet over the top to make the noise and draw inquisitive fish down. This way, your pile of groundbait on the bottom will really stand out.

Margins

The second area to target big fish on hard days is the margins. At some point the cruising fish will disappear and begin to mooch around the margins for food. This can often be triggered by wind, a change in temperature, or is due to the time of day. On some sessions it will happen after a couple of hours, while on others it will happen in the last 30 minutes. Still, you need to be prepared, as two or three extra fish from here can add 40lb or more to your weight. On this particular lake, I've gone from coming nowhere to having more than 100lb in the last hour down the edge to win.

I see many anglers piling bait down both edges, but feel that this splits up the fish and creates an element of doubt in your head. If one side isn't working, you're constantly thinking that there could be fish down the other. My advice is to pick the best margin and feed just that spot. For big carp I look for a sensible depth of two and a half feet on a clean, hard and preferably flat bottom. I'm only expecting one or two fish to come in at a time, so liners from having lots of small fish in the peg shouldn't be a problem. Today I've chosen to fish just short of the next platform to my right. There's a slight breeze coming from the left, so by fishing this way I'll also be able to gain better presentation, without the float constantly blowing back under the pole.

Strong Gear

Those anglers who know me always say I fish very heavy.

This skimmer was first to show… before the big boys turned up!

Buoyant-bristled floats with plenty of weight are the order of the day.

This isn't always the case, but in circumstances where bites from very big fish are few and far between, I don't believe scaling down makes any difference. On the Method feeder there's no way of nicely presenting a bait by having a slow fall, so I opt to set a trap with strong gear on. I'd sooner not get a bite from a fish than hook one and lose it. Main line is 8lb Daiwa ST mono. This is super-durable, highly abrasive resistant, and sinks like a brick. A bow can lead to the feeder moving as the line is sinking. This moves the hook bait out of the feeder and potentially ruins my trap! The hooklength is four inches of 0.22mm line to a size 12 QM1 hook with a hair rig.

My pole gear follows the same trend – strength being my key focus. Elastic is purple Hydro – forgiving but powerful. This will allow me to land fish quickly if they suddenly turn up with little time to go. I fish straight through down the margins to minimise weak spots in the rig. Line is 0.20mm tied to a size

12 Gamakatsu Carp hook. For the margins I use some old Mick Wilkinson floats that are more than 10 years old. They take around six No8 shot, which are bulked around a foot from the hook. This ensures that my hook bait is nailed in position when a carp comes along.

Baits

A brilliant method over the last two years has involved feeding groundbait down the edge. This has started to work really well here at Gold Valley, although I've tweaked it a little to make it extra effective. Groundbait choice is really important. Anything too fine, or too fishmeal and pellet oriented, will lead to fish becoming preoccupied. I'm using the Specimen Carp mix from Old Ghost. This contains some fishmeal, but is made up of very big particles that will hold on the bottom and prevent the carp from 'gill feeding'. To this I also add half a bag of Maggot Meal. This is made up of all kinds of maggot-based attractors, and you can actually see the skins and dried-out maggots within it! It pays to mix the groundbait well before use so that it remains dead on the bottom; mixing it on the damp side will also help this.

The next trick comes when I add some feed to the mix. Many anglers simply cup in loose groundbait. I think this is far too negative, and leads to the carp ignoring any 'solid' hook baits you present over the top. Today I've added a full tin of sweetcorn, and a pint of dead red maggots to the mix. These stand out like a beacon on the bottom and create plenty of particles to hold the carp. Rather than cup the groundbait in loose, I like to give it a quick nip together. This will immediately bread up on the bottom but gives me the confidence that everything gets down. If I were fishing in really shallow water or on a slope, I might cup in an overwetted, loose mix.

My Method groundbait is super simple, consisting of one bag of the same Specimen Carp mix. The big particles create a nice balance between pellets and groundbait, and crumble away from the Method very quickly so the carp can get at the bait!

Making It Work

At the start of the session I cupped in three balls of my margin mix, lightly nipped together. However, I'm going to begin with a patient Method attack. I've seen anglers waste a match chasing cruising carp, and would much rather try to catch the odd one that actually wants to feed. The carp in here average 6lb to 10lb, with many well into double figures. I only need to catch 10 10lb fish over five hours

| *You need strong gear for carp!*

Method fishing can be a real waiting game – two rests are essential.

Using the right gear means that big fish can be subdued very quickly.

and I'll have 100lb. I've clipped up inline with a buoy on the rope, and begin with an 8mm banded pellet on the hook.

It's vital to be confident that you've got everything right when waiting on the Method. I lightly bury my hook bait in the groundbait and, after using a mould to form a neat pile, give it a good squeeze by hand to ensure it doesn't break off the feeder on impact. Casting out and sitting for spells of 15 minutes before recasting is often my ploy. Hitting the clip with the rod to one side cushions the feeder in, allowing you to follow it forward onto the rest. This way the feeder hits the bottom directly below where it's landed.

Make sure your box setup is very comfortable, and use both a front and butt rest. This way the rod is free from any movements you make. Anglers with the rod across their knee are more inclined to move the feeder, and pick up at false bites.

After an hour's fishing I haven't had a proper bite. The carp are still cruising and every now and again I get a big liner as one drags over my line. Changing to a bright white pellet hook bait brings an instant bite but, rather than being the big carp I'm after, it's a skimmer of around 2lb! However, three carp in the next hour, all approaching double figures, make the wait worthwhile. These have all come on white or red pellet hook baits, which stand out on the feeder like a beacon. It's also noticeable that the bites come after the feeder has been in the water for at least 10 minutes. At the halfway stage the gentle breeze seems to pick up, and turns directly towards my bank. This makes my margin attack increasingly favourable, and I've been potting in the occasional ball down there every 30 minutes. The cruising fish seem to have disappeared, which is a sign they're thinking about feeding, so it's time to have a go!

I cup in another ball of the mix, and bait up with my favourite margin hook bait – eight dead red maggots! This big, visual bait is devastating for big carp. Double particle baits are also very good, being slightly heavier if there are several big fish wafting around in the swim. Double corn is a particular favourite of mine. I lower the rig over the feed, getting a nerve-provoking wobble on the float as the bait settles. A few seconds later my thick bristle whacks under, and several feet of purple Hydro is dragged from the pole tip with the angry headshakes of a Gold Valley lump! I ship back to the top kit as quickly as possible, and, by keeping the tip low, a common of 12lb is in the pan in less than a minute. Another ball of the mix is cupped in before the same happens again, with a 10lb fish being the culprit! The cruising fish have obviously decided to feed, and by sticking to my guns with this simple approach, I've enjoyed an amazing final two hours.

A dozen big carp, along with the handful of fish on the Method, have given me a weight approaching 150lb. Many anglers would have spent today chasing fish around and flitting between different methods. With this super-positive approach on days like this, you'll come out on top every time!

Just part of the 150lb net that Will caught with his positive but simple approach!